PRAISE FOR *JUST ASK US*
SPEAK OUT ON STUDENT ENGAGEMENT

Just Ask Us: Kids Speak Out on Student Engagement *is an outstanding resource manual for teachers to increase student engagement. Each chapter includes extensive quotes from students that support researched-based best practices. Diagrams and photos of student work illustrate how students can effectively work together and use more visually stimulating methods to connect their learning to real-world applications.*

**Mary Ann Burke, EdD, Author,
Trainer, and Co-Founder
Generational Parenting Blog at
GenParenting.com
San Jose, CA**

Heather Wolpert-Gawron meshes her teaching experience with extensive student feedback to offer sage advice and a clear argument as to the importance of increased student engagement within their learning environments. She provides practical application that will help teachers everywhere up their game in providing students the right foundation for deeper connections to their learning.

**Janelle McLaughlin, Educational Consultant
Innovative Education Solutions
Manchester, IN**

Just Ask Us: Kids Speak Out on Student Engagement *is not only a quality read but also a fresh perspective beyond just providing interesting lessons. It clearly states that student engagement is directly connected to academic content and outcomes.*

**Julie Frederick, Nationally Board
Certified Kindergarten Teacher
Broadview Thomson K–8
Seattle WA**

Any teacher who ever wanted to poll students about what works best for them when learning, and then really use that data to help students, should read this book. The research behind WHY the ideas presented work, and the practical strategies suggested, are also great bonuses.

**Patrick Pergola, 7th Grade Science Teacher
Sparta Middle School
Sparta, NJ**

JUST ASK US

To Addie Holsing

For decades, you engaged students. Then you moved on and mentored teachers like me. May you now be engaging the angels themselves.

JUST ASK US

KIDS SPEAK OUT ON STUDENT ENGAGEMENT

HEATHER WOLPERT-GAWRON

FOREWORD BY CAROL RADFORD

A JOINT PUBLICATION

A SAGE Publishing Company

FOR INFORMATION:

Corwin
A SAGE Company
2455 Teller Road
Thousand Oaks, California 91320
(800) 233-9936
www.corwin.com

SAGE Publications Ltd.
1 Oliver's Yard
55 City Road
London EC1Y 1SP
United Kingdom

SAGE Publications India Pvt. Ltd.
B 1/I 1 Mohan Cooperative Industrial Area
Mathura Road, New Delhi 110 044
India

SAGE Publications Asia-Pacific Pte. Ltd.
3 Church Street
#10-04 Samsung Hub
Singapore 049483

Acquisitions Editor: Ariel Bartlett
Senior Developmental Editor: Desirée A. Bartlett
Editorial Assistant: Kaitlyn Irwin
Production Editor: Bennie Clark Allen
Copy Editor: Lana Todorovic-Arndt
Typesetter: C&M Digitals (P) Ltd.
Proofreader: Rae-Ann Goodwin
Indexer: Jeanne Busemeyer
Cover Designer: Janet Kiesel
Marketing Manager: Anna Mesick

Printed in the United States of America

ISBN: 978-1-5063-6328-8

This book is printed on acid-free paper.

Certified Chain of Custody
Promoting Sustainable Forestry
www.sfiprogram.org
SFI-01268

SFI label applies to text stock

17 18 19 20 21 10 9 8 7 6 5 4 3 2 1

CONTENTS

FOREWORD

My first experience with asking students what they thought of my teaching happened quite by accident. I was in my beginning years of teaching fifth grade and was frustrated that the students were not engaged. In fact, they were so distracted that I couldn't hear myself teach! So I loudly asked, "Well, what do you think I should be doing?" Silence. They couldn't believe I asked them. Then they authentically shared what I could do to engage them and how I could be a better teacher. I never looked back. I continually sought out ways to find out what my students thought. I used informal surveys, tickets to leave, and even had students draw pictures of me teaching so I could see what I looked like in the classroom.

Later in my career as a teacher educator I discovered that novice teachers were still facing the same challenges. In one of our class discussions a teacher shared that he had a student who changed her math grade from an F to an A! We wanted to know how this teacher had helped the student succeed in school. We decided to ask Jennifer, the high school student, and record her responses. My first video, *Teachers Make a Difference,* was produced and shared in all of our teacher education courses. I was hooked!

We continued our research, asking students, "What is an effective teacher?" and "What advice would you give beginning teachers?" We created online surveys, designed protocols for novice teachers and mentors to talk about the data, and produced a series of student perspectives videos. We learned that students had opinions about how their teachers could teach them more effectively. We also learned that novice teachers wanted to change their practices so their students could succeed.

What was missing in my journey into student perspectives was specific ways the novices could actually "engage" their students. That is why I am so excited about this book, ***Just Ask Us: Kids Speak Out On Student Engagement***. Heather Wolpert-Gawron is an experienced practicing teacher. She has done her research, collected student voices from across the nation, and tested the practices in her own classroom. She includes a Student Engagement Survey in the introduction to help you get started with these ideas in your own classrooms right now.

If the goal is to help our students learn and be successful in school, then we need to listen to them. We need to pay attention to what they need, not what we think they need.

Heather has brilliantly captured the essence of students' perspectives in each chapter. She has learned that students want to

- *work together,*
- *have their teachers be more visual and to use technology,*
- *know "why" they are learning,*
- *move around in the classroom,*
- *have choices,*
- *experience their teachers as human,*
- *create using what they know,*
- *participate with new ways of learning, and*
- *learn using a variety of methods.*

These specific topics come from the students' voices and Heather organizes them into separate chapters that include samples and many choices for engaging our students. What I love most about this book is that all these creative ideas are in one place, and the format is easy to read, making it useful for busy teachers.

I agree with what Heather says at the end of the book:

> *Without engagement, your students cannot absorb your content. Without engagement, your students will not be willing to go through the steps of the learning process. Without engagement, your students will not be on your side, and you are a vital ally in their development.*

Most of my current work relates to transforming education for students by supporting novice teachers and their mentors. Mentoring relationships invite us to be open to another person's perspective. They require us to listen and be nonjudgmental. The students who are the heart of this book *are our mentors.* They are helping us to grow and improve our teaching methods. We just have to listen.

I wish I had this book when I was teaching in my very first classroom and when I was preparing teacher candidates. I do know I will recommend it to the mentors and novice teachers in my current mentoring courses. We all want to see our students change their grades from an F to an A like Jennifer did.

Heather's experience, enthusiasm, and creativity offer us a way to make a difference in our interactions with students. That is why ***Just Ask Us: Kids Speak Out On Student Engagement*** is such an important book for all teachers. Thank you, Heather, for sharing students' voices with us so we can all learn from their wisdom.

Carol Radford, EdD
Founder and CEO, MentoringinAction.com
Author, *Mentoring in Action: Guiding Sharing and Reflecting With Novice Teachers* and
The First Years Matter: Becoming an Effective Teacher

ACKNOWLEDGMENTS

M any thanks to all of the engaging teachers who contributed to this book. You are teachers that students remember. I believe that if every adult in this generation had been assigned to your classrooms as children, school would be remembered only with joy. Thanks in particular to Susie Aames, Jason Trapp, Sheryl Nussbaum-Beach, Trevor Hershberger, Liz Harrington, Jim Bentley, Diane Tom, Michael Corso, Rich Lehrer, Eric Hoenigmann, and Jennifer Trapp. Many thanks also to my own network of teachers that supports me every day: my beloved Writing Project and the educators from the George Lucas Educational Foundation's Edutopia.org. Deep thanks to my own school district, San Gabriel Unified, to Jefferson Middle School, and in particular to my principal, Matt Arnold, who supports student engagement as if it were a core subject itself. Finally, many thanks to the amazing teachers and their students who contributed to the Student Engagement Survey. Your responses made this book possible.

Corwin gratefully acknowledges the contributions of the following reviewers:

Betty Brandenburg, Consultant/Retired Educator
Department of Defense Education Activity
Fort Knox, KY

Donna Eurich, Middle School ELA Advanced IB
St. Ann Catholic School
West Palm Beach, FL

Julie Frederick, Nationally Board Certified Kindergarten Teacher
Broadview Thomson K–8
Seattle, WA

Lisa Graham, Director, Special Education
Berkeley Unified School District
Berkeley, CA

Maria Langworthy, Senior Program Officer
Bill and Melinda Gates Foundation
Seattle, WA

Jan McClaren, Educator
Claremore High School
Claremore, OK

Janelle McLaughlin, Educational Consultant
Innovative Education Solutions
North Manchester, IN

Lyneille Meza, Director of Data and Assessment
Denton Independent School District
Denton, TX

Patrick Pergola, Seventh-Grade Science Teacher
Sparta Middle School
Sparta, NJ

Ernie Rambo, Teacher
Walter Johnson Jr. High School
Las Vegas, NV

Tim Tharrington, Sixth-Grade English Teacher
Wakefield Middle School
Raleigh, NC

Leonard J. Villanueva, Elementary School Teacher
Palisades Elementary School
Pearl City, HI

ABOUT THE AUTHOR

Heather Wolpert-Gawron is an award-winning middle school teacher. She is a staff blogger for Edutopia.org and shares all things middle school at tweenteacher .com. She has been a proud member of the California Writing Project since 2008. She is the author of the following books: *DIY for Project Based Learning for ELA and History, DIY for Project Based Learning for Math and Science, Writing Behind Every Door: Teaching Common Core Writing in the Content Areas* and *'Tween Crayons and Curfews: Tips for Middle School Teachers.* Heather is passionate about project-based learning and believes the Maker Movement for teachers is in curriculum design. Heather believes curriculum design itself should tell a story, and she helps her students craft the tale. Heather lives with her husband and two boys in Los Angeles where they play Dungeons & Dragons every week, building their cross-over stories and adventures together. Follow Heather on Twitter: @tweenteacher.

Photo courtesy of Davis Lester

INTRODUCTION

THE IMPORTANCE OF STUDENT ENGAGEMENT

How important is it that a middle schooler or high schooler be engaged with what we are teaching? Why must they enjoy it and connect with the material in order to embed it? The answer to these questions can be seen in every classroom, in every school. Engagement isn't just about fun: It's about functionality. It isn't just about laughter: It's about ensuring there is a joy in learning.

Kelly Gallagher, author of *Readicide* and *Write Like This*, insists that engagement must happen before we can imagine students deeply absorbing content; and only after that can we begin to discuss elevating our subject to reflect more rigorous content. In other words, engagement must be the starting line for any academic marathon.

However, as any teacher or parent knows, tweens and teens are a hard group to engage. According to Raleigh Philip (2006), author of *Engaging 'Tweens and Teens*, "Teachers often make assumptions that their directions have gotten through. But the disconnect is that the student often doesn't get it. His or her interpretation is really different."

For this reason, we have to work harder to get it right. Our instincts as educators may not be totally on-point, and we must align our assumptions with the reality of what our students really need.

A classroom that is focused just as much on engagement as it is on academic achievement not only runs smoother, but also achieves an overall goal that should function as a teacher's target. "That never-ending mark," to quote Shakespeare, that unwavering target, should be in developing people who appreciate lifelong learning. After all, enjoying school doesn't end when our students leave our schools' walls. The joy of learning should be a cushion that carries students into higher education and beyond.

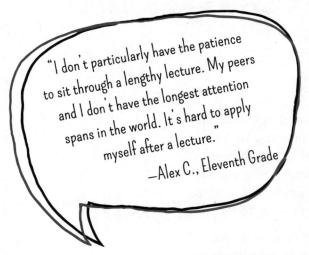

"I don't particularly have the patience to sit through a lengthy lecture. My peers and I don't have the longest attention spans in the world. It's hard to apply myself after a lecture."

—Alex C., Eleventh Grade

Developing positive memories of our school years helps our children as they travel the roads of adulthood, and they even pass that enthusiasm on to their own children, students that many of us might one day see in our own classrooms. These children sit in the chairs of their relatives, and they come with opinions of both you and learning in general. Will they arrive with prejudices about the learning process that are good or bad? Will they have been told stories about a classroom where their interests and engagement were a focus? Will they enter our rooms with eagerness that what they will be learning will be meaningful?

Being engaged in learning opens up the brain to receive both quantitatively and qualitatively. Engagement opens up the door to deeper learning.

QUANTIFYING STUDENT ENGAGEMENT

The group of teachers met four times a year in an EdCamp style of collaboration. This group's focus was on project-based learning. I had been brought in to moderate an informal discussion and provide resources if necessary. In the corner sat the dreaded "third-grade team" who had made it clear that there were no strategies mentioned that could work with this year's group of students.

"There's no way this could work with our students this year," the lead teacher said. "They're crazy. Just crazy. You don't even understand what this group is like."

Another nodded in agreement and added, "None of them listen. They don't follow directions. There's no way we can have them collaborate in groups because they won't even do the work we tell them to do individually."

"And they're never quiet!" another teacher in the group said. "They always want to talk!"

"I wonder," I mused. "How many kids are we talking about? I mean the ones that are 'crazy'? Are we talking, say, 50% of your students that are difficult?"

"At least!" she said.

"So, let's talk numbers here. If 50% of your 30 students aren't responding to the strategies you're currently using, maybe they need other strategies?"

When pressed, they shared that their current strategies to help students with their lack of focus included seating them in rows to control the talking in the room and utilizing curriculum largely dictated by textbook reading and workbook pages. They felt the students couldn't be trusted with other ways to learn the material.

I nodded my understanding. "It's true. Some classes are more difficult than others. But what would the numbers of 'harder students' look like if you leveraged some of their tendencies?" I created a list of structured suggestions that helped quantify what their classroom might look like if they brought in different engagement strategies. Here's what I offered:

> ***Heterogeneously grouping kids in collaborative groups**: I suggested nine groups made up of three to four students. That disperses the most concerning students and gives them the chance to work with kids who follow the directions given. They agreed that while this wouldn't work to solve all of the problems, it might help five of the 15 difficult students.

> ***Using technology in a structured and consistent way**: I suggested using Brainpop once a week (Monday, to introduce a concept), using Padlet twice a week (Tuesday and Thursday, as an exit card at the end of class), and developing a Kahoot game (Friday, as an informal

(Continued)

(Continued)

assessment of the students' knowledge). I also suggested the teachers collaborate themselves and split the responsibility of creating the weekly Kahoot game to share the burden. The teachers agreed, especially coming from a place of using no technology at all, that this might help five more students.

***Giving students choice**: I suggested that they allow students to select how they want to share what they know about the upcoming unit's topic. I showed them Google Slides, Powtoons, and a rubric on Oral Presentation, as well as a more traditional outline for a written assignment. The teachers felt that might pull in two more students from that initial group.*

***Having more 1:1 time with those students who really are struggling with learning for reasons that might be beyond your control**: I stressed that there are kids in every class that will be challenging; there may not be a way around that, and many times they do need extra attention. But it's just as important to weed out students who are simply not engaged. And to do that requires our efforts in engaging them.*

"I mean, what we're talking about here," I said, "is student engagement. The kids are desperate to be pulled into the content, and if we aren't working to keep them engaged with more than just the subject and our delivery of it, then I guess you're right; there becomes a tipping point of 'crazy.'"

Engaging students not only helps them love to learn, but it helps us love to teach. We all entered this profession excited to spark an interest in learning, to see that light bulb pop with excitement over a student's head. That can only happen if we put effort into engaging the students before us.

PEDAGOGY VERSUS PERSONALITY

But many teachers confuse entertainment with engagement, and for that reason, we find some educators reluctant to move beyond familiar lessons or structures. After all, being on stage all day is exhausting, so I want to debunk that assumption right away. Engagement is different from making everything "fun." It is not our job to put on a top hat and do a soft shoe to get the kids' attention. This book is not about making the argument that our job is to somehow get students to laugh all the time or be entertained by their teachers.

That's too heavy a burden, and I think we can all agree that this is not the message we want school to send. Not everything in life, whether in school or outside its walls, must be entertaining to be valuable. Nevertheless, when we are learning, we must be engaged. We must find a way to have the lessons stick. The students must be alert and must be willing to open their minds and hearts to learning. This book focuses on strategies that can help you do that without choreographing a dance number to keep the kids smiling.

When I think of engagement, I don't think of "fun." I think of all elements as "engaging," as in all elements coming together and ready to go. I think of Captain Picard and his "Engage!" before the Enterprise speeds off to an adventure. I think of trains coupling before being pulled and picking up steam. Engagement isn't always about what makes a kid smile; it's about engaging the machine that is the brain, and activating everything, not because it has to, but because the student wants it to. It isn't about easy or fun. It's about willingness to work and triggering the ability to connect with the learning.

Many teachers also are engaging simply by the mere power of their personality. We all know these educators. For some, it is their personas that get them by. However, they too need to ensure that their personalities are combining with pedagogy in order to prepare their students for any personality they may meet in the future.

And even the kids know the difference. If a teacher doesn't have the content knowledge to back up the smile or stories, kids will become wise to the facade. Having said that, kids also know when their smile means the world to you.

Teaching using the strategies of engagement, therefore, helps to level the playing field. In other words, being engaging is learnable. Keeping students engaged in their learning is something every teacher can do.

> "Engagement isn't about easy or fun. It's about willingness to work and triggering the ability to connect with the learning."

> "What engages me is how much the teacher knows their job *and* how spritely the teacher is. There has to be a balance between the two."
>
> —Teagan S., Eighth Grade

AN ARGUMENT: WHAT ENGAGES
TEACHERS ALSO ENGAGES STUDENTS

I believe that we, the educators, are not so different from our young clientele. After all, it's possible that there is no great mystery as to what engages students because what engages students is what engages every learner, no matter their place in life.

Think about the following questions and see if your responses align with some of the chapter headings in this very book.

1. When you are at a faculty meeting, what frustrates you the most?

2. What is the best professional development experience you've had? What were the qualities of the moderator or leader?

3. What was your worst professional development experience you've had? What were the qualities of both the facilitator and the material?

4. In what way do you like your material delivered? What helps you digest information the most efficiently and in a way that "sticks"?

5. In what way do you most like to report what you know? If you had the choice of presenting your knowledge orally, written, recorded, and so on, which would you, prefer? Do you like having the choice to begin with?

6. When you sit on a committee at a school or outside organization, do you like to take on all of the tasks yourself, or do you like things delegated to others as well?

7. What kinds of assessments do you like to review once the students have taken them? That is, are there assessments you dread having to score, or are there ones you look forward to spending time grading? Case in point, my department used to assign a persuasive writing Benchmark about the debate surrounding the need to keep the penny. *Should the penny be taken out of our monetary system?* The essays we read, hundreds of them, could put an entire department to sleep. Believe me; I've seen it. But a few years later, we changed that same assessment and asked students to hunt through some resources on the grossest jobs around.

They then had to write a cover letter for one of the jobs as if they were applying for it. The scoring of those essays was almost a pleasure (save for having to read about some really gross jobs). So I would ask again: Think about the tests or assignments you don't mind spending time reviewing over your own coffee table at home. Which ones do you prefer? I would argue that if you are engaged reading them, the students were probably engaged developing them.

I would also make the argument that many tweens and teens would answer these questions in a way that is similar to you. Of course, because they are in a different chapter of life, that can make a difference. After all, their brains are wired slightly differently than those of an adult.

> "If you are engaged reading them, the students were probably engaged developing them."

A BRIEF NOTE ON BRAIN RESEARCH AND STUDENT ENGAGEMENT

When the brain is stimulated, that is, when the brain is engaged, something amazing happens. It not only lights up, its neurons firing with connections, but it begins to absorb material in a deeper way.

There are strategies that teachers can use to tickle the higher cognitive functioning of our brains in such a way that both hemispheres are triggered. There are strategies that improve language acquisition, brain development, and social interaction.

In addition, a classroom that can provide multiple strategies of teaching can also help encourage the dendrites of the brain to connect and form networks that can help with memory and critical thinking. Providing a variety of strategies in a classroom increases learning.

Admittedly, when it comes to the brain, engagement isn't just about interest; it's also about enjoyment. When we enjoy what we are doing, dopamine is released into our brains. This dopamine has been shown to click "save" on information as we discover it. In other words, if a student has an enjoyable memory associated with the learning of information, that knowledge is more likely to be stored in long-term memory than discarded into the short-term memory bin.

Unfortunately, educational policymakers many times don't make decisions based on brain research. If they did, they would know that an engaged class is a class of deeper learning. And that the sounds and sights of engagement, while not always traditional or solemn, indicate knowledge acquisition that is bound to embed information more successfully.

Dr. Judy Willis (n.d.), the neurologist-turned-second-grade-teacher-turned-middle-school- teacher says the following in an article for *Psychology Today*:

> In their zeal to raise test scores, too many policymakers wrongly assume that students who are laughing, interacting in groups, or being creative with art, music, or dance are not doing real academic work. The result is that some teachers feel pressure to preside over more sedate classrooms with students on the same page in the same book, sitting in straight rows, facing straight ahead. The truth is that when we scrub joy and comfort from the classroom, we distance our students from effective information processing and long-term memory storage . . . research suggests that superior learning takes place when classroom experiences are enjoyable . . . when classroom activities are pleasurable, the brain releases dopamine, a neurotransmitter that stimulates the memory centers and promotes the release of acetylcholinem, which increases focused attention.

"The truth is that when we scrub joy and comfort from the classroom, we distance our students from effective information processing and long-term memory storage."

—Dr. Judy Willis

It all boils down to boredom. Boredom, as it turns out, isn't just an energy sucker, it's a brainpower sucker, too. In other words, if a student is bored, a cycle can begin where the brain becomes less able to re-engage.

"Bored people are less invested in learning, challenging themselves, and growing," says Todd Kashdan (2010), Professor of Psychology at George Mason University in his article for *The Huffington Post*:

> In turn, the natural brain degeneration that occurs as we age is likely to speed up. This is because as we attend to novelty, manage novelty, and extract rewards from novel and challenging situations, we build and strengthen existing neuron connections in our brain.

> Yep, you can die of boredom. Or, at least, an underengaged student can certainly feel like it and become detached from learning.

Therefore, we must help engage our students. But the question is, How? What strategies work best in engaging them?

The answer is simple. Ask them.

Throughout this book, you'll see QR codes that take you to videos of teachers utilizing these strategies in their classroom. You might see a high school math teacher guiding students to work in collaborative groups or a middle school language arts teacher allowing students to move around the classroom with a purpose. Feel free to explore these links as you read along or archive them for future examples as you consider your own lesson design. This textbox is an example of what you'll see peppered throughout this book. Think of these videos as supplemental material to help enhance your learning journey through this process.

Video 0.1 Just Ask Them

ENGAGE WITH THE CONTENT!

This video footage introduces you to some of the overall concepts you'll see as you progress through the book. You'll also be introduced to just some of the students you'll meet throughout this book, and you'll hear firsthand how vital engagement strategies can be. You'll also see your first window into some classrooms that will be featured in more detail in later chapters. See if you can spot the following:

- Technology use
- Verbal communication between students
- Visuals to enhance comprehension
- Kids moving around
- And more!

THE ENGAGEMENT SURVEY PROCESS

Throughout a school year, teachers are asked to identify, define, and analyze our students, our lessons, our units, and our pedagogy. We puzzle through problems indicated by student behavior and lack of academic achievement. We seek solutions as to why this lesson was effective over that one, or that student succeeded while another failed. We call in the parents. We reach out to counselors. We attend conferences.

But we are going about this all wrong. What we really need to do is ask the students themselves.

My student, Sharon, Grade 8, said it well when she stated,

> The thing is, every student is engaged differently, but that is okay. There is always a way to keep a student interested and lively, ready to embark on the journey of education. "What is that way?" some teachers may ask eagerly. Now, read closely. Are you ready? That way is to ask them. Ask. Them. Get their input on how they learn. It's just as simple as that.

So that's what I did in 2011 to all 220 of my language arts students. I created a survey using SurveyMonkey and began to devise a way to crack the code of student engagement. I thought long and hard about how to approach my students in a way that could bring out the most honest and straightforward responses. I developed my inquiry and launched my complex survey.

Ready to know how I got their responses? Ready to know what I asked? Here goes: "What engages students?" That's it. Three words. No more, no less.

And from that one simple question, there emerged responses that clearly reflected a series of nine major categories, themes that began to rise up from the abyss of answers. These themes have become signposts for my own practice ever since, and I shared them in a post I wrote for the George Lucas Educational Foundation's Edutopia later that year ("Kids Speak Out on Student Engagement," 2012).

Five years later, the original Edutopia post has been shared through social media almost 50,000 times. And each year since that first survey was conducted, I brush off my poll and survey a new crop of students to make sure my own practice is calibrated to the new students before me.

With each school year, I find that the students from years ago have much in common with their current peers. "Kids these days," as the old kvetch states, simply doesn't apply; the kids polled most recently tend to agree with their counterparts I surveyed years ago.

This book not only shares my findings from all of the surveys over the years, it adds more recent responses from hundreds more. During the spring of 2015, I sent out the same survey via Twitter, Facebook, and other social media. The George Lucas Educational Foundation's Edutopia shared it through their Twitter feed, as did Corwin. For this book, I expanded the reach of my survey to include middle schoolers and high schoolers from across the nation, from rural areas to urban ones, from coast to coast. I received input from classes of honors students to classes of special education students, from English language learners to English-only students. There are results from Title I schools and charter schools, from public schools and private schools, from traditional institutions to progressive ones.

The amazing thing was this—even after expanding the survey beyond my own classroom's walls, even after almost a decade later, the student responses fell under the same familiar categories.

They make up the chapters in this book and are as follows:

1. Let Us Work Together

2. Make Learning More Visual and Utilize Technology

3. Connect What We Learn to the Real World

4. Let Us Move Around

5. Give Us Choices

6. Show Us You're Human Too

7. Help Us Create Something With What We've Learned

8. Teach Us Something New in a New Way

9. Mix Things Up

These are the voices of students who will one day be our politicians, our lawyers, our mechanics, our programmers, our doctors, our waiters, our clerks, our protesters, our accountants, our artists, and our whatever-profession-we-can't-yet-name. Nevertheless, they all agree on what engages them as learners.

The survey has confirmed that students want to learn. When asked, "What engages students?" kids rarely answer whimsically and never with the response, "I'm engaged when things are easy." If anything, many acknowledge that a challenge can be engaging.

Additionally, students seemed to appreciate being asked the question, and in the case of my students, I saw students who, at times, reluctantly participate, engage greatly in the survey itself knowing it was being read and deeply considered.

For this book, I polled approximately 1,500 students and have compiled a new list, one not much different from the list years back, that includes some additional themes as well. I've included quotes from the students themselves, and in addition, I have included input from teachers as to how these concepts can become a part of one's classroom environment.

For those newer to teaching, I encourage you to begin down a road paved in engagement. For those who have been around the block already, take the time to survey your own class or continue the practice of surveying with each year so that you can see if trends ebb and flow with our students.

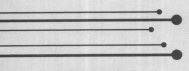

ENGAGE WITH THE CONTENT!

This video includes more details about the difference between engagement and fun. Sure, there's a correlation between the words, and they are related, but the two words are not synonyms.

As you watch the video, notice the similarities between the concepts both students and teachers are referring to.

Think about what engages you as a learner yourself and how you can leverage what you know about teacher engagement into your classroom of students.

Video 0.2 Does Engagement Equal Fun?

HOW IS THIS BOOK DIFFERENT FROM OTHERS?

Just Ask Us: Kids Speak Out on Student Engagement is a unique book that reflects the results of a national survey of students in Grades 6–12. The results of this survey align with a short list of vital and research-based strategies that teachers can bring into their classrooms.

However, it's important to note two things:

1. Each topic in this book can, in fact, be its own book. Each strategy can be justified by research found in white papers, articles, books, and dissertations. Think of this

book as yet another rationale as to why it's vital to utilize these strategies. Think of this book as an *amuse-bouche* of strategies, a little taste that is meant to introduce you to concepts and give you short, practical takeaways to try immediately. Dive deeply into some of the mentioned strategies by furthering your research, or simply dip your toe into other methods after reading these chapters.

2. All of these categories bleed into each other. They all wrap together and braid. For example, being a teacher who isn't nervous about showing his or her humanity and flaws *does* build community in the overall classroom. Embedding technology *can* be a form of bringing in visuals into a lesson or mixing up the way in which information is delivered or accepted. Giving students choice can include collaboration. Encouraging students to create something with what they've learned *is* project-based learning and can connect to the real world. Nevertheless, I've teased these topics apart because the students did or, conversely, blended concepts based on students' tendencies to mash-up strategies. For example, many students begged to use technology because it was so visual. Others mentioned project-based learning because it was meaningful.

So what this book does is tease apart each topic, based on how a student views them. In so doing, I'm hoping that they are each easier to deconstruct for the teacher who is new to learning them.

For those who are not new to these strategies, I hope this book encourages you to look at the students before you, year after year, and defer to their knowledge of how they learn best. After all, what's most engaging to you might not be the strategy engaging to most of your students. On the other hand, you might find some strategies many students claim to love, but it will be up to you to introduce them to others. It only happens if you ask them.

This book shares the results of the survey through direct, unedited, quotes from the students themselves. Each chapter also provides how different teachers, in both middle and high school, and in many different subjects, achieve these goals.

Another supplemental element to this book is the companion website where you will find downloadables as well as links to videos mentioned in the book. There are layers of materials provided to help make this journey helpful and, dare I say, engaging.

"Think of this book as an *amuse-bouche* of strategies, a little taste that is meant to introduce you to concepts and give you short, practical takeaways to try immediately."

"Our directive comes not
from federal mandate,
the state standards, the
Common Core standards,
curricular fads, or district
desires. It comes from what
one might call the Student
Standards."

The companion website can be found at http://resources.corwin
.com/justaskus.

This book helps to guide teachers by honoring the voices of the
students we serve. Our directive comes not from federal mandate,
the state standards, the Common Core standards, curricular fads,
or district desires. It comes from what one might call the Student
Standards.

This book has been written, indirectly at least, by students
themselves. It is being compiled based on their opinions and
written with their input, and they have helped pen the concepts
within it. They have driven the chapter headings. They have
driven the curating of ideas.

Students are vital stakeholders that are very rarely asked for their
input in their own learning process. This book embraces their
opinions of how they learn best, and it validates not only their
ideas, but also the strategies others have claimed to be effective.

This book isn't about theory, but about implementation. It's about
Monday, not someday. Our students have spoken, and we must
heed their input.

STUDENT ENGAGEMENT SURVEY

FULL NAME:

TEACHER NAME:

Before you answer the following question, think about what excites you to learn and to show your learning. Think about what you like about your classes, even if the subject isn't your favorite. Ready for the question?

What engages you?

_____

_____

_____

_____

_____

_____

As a follow up, think about the most engaging lesson or activity or assignment that you have had in school. Be specific and describe this lesson or assignment.

_____

_____

_____

_____

_____

_____

Circle the following tags that perhaps best represent what engages you most about that lesson or assignment. Does that lesson utilize any or all of the following?:

Tags: Visuals, Technology, Project-Based Learning, Real-World Applications, Group Work (Collaboration), Creating/Making, Movement, Student Choice, a Variety of Styles, Teacher Enthusiasm

You never know what you can do until you Try

CHAPTER ONE

LET US WORK TOGETHER

"I feel stronger working in groups . . ."

OVERVIEW

No response appeared in the student engagement survey with more frequency than that of getting to collaborate, talk, and work with their peers. Period.

Regardless of their age or region, the students who were surveyed insisted that this one strategy drew them into learning deeper than

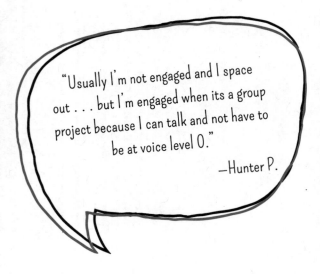

"Usually I'm not engaged and I space out . . . but I'm engaged when its a group project because I can talk and not have to be at voice level 0."

—Hunter P.

any other method. And it's no surprise. After all, the research shows this to be true as well.

According to Linda Darling-Hammond and Brigid Barron in their 2012 post for Edutopia, "Research Supports Collaborative Learning," their studies proved "how group work supports individual learning, such as resolving differing perspectives through argument, explaining one's thinking, observing the strategies of others, and listening to explanations." By having access to these different perspectives, studies show that individual learning increases.

In other words, studies have shown multiple reasons why cooperative learning has proven so successful:

1. There is an increase in achievement because there is group motivation to succeed. Some activities can focus on reward brought on by group growth and accomplishment.

2. There is an increase in achievement because of the care that develops between the members of the group. This care proves to be an authentic motivator in helping one another.

3. There is an increase in achievement because of interactions between students. Mental processing of information is different in groups than by individuals alone. Cooperative learning improves both cognitive and developmental goals for individual students. (Slavin, 1996)

And this increase applies to a variety of students. Collaboration has proven, time and again, to benefit all levels of learners. Robert E. Slavin (1996) of Johns Hopkins University reports that "[o]ne 2-year study of schools using cooperative learning most of their instructional day found that high, average, and low achievers all achieved better than controls at similar achievement levels." By explaining concepts to lower learners, the higher learners prove to embed knowledge further, while the lower learners benefit from the expertise at the table.

Kagan Online Magazine compiled further research on cooperative grouping and its correlation with student achievement, and reports that,

In 67 studies of the achievement effects of cooperative learning 61% found significantly greater achievement in cooperative than in traditionally taught control groups. Positive effects were found in all major subjects, all grade levels, in urban, rural, and suburban schools, and for high, average, and low achievers. (Dotson, 2001)

But research in the learning outcomes of cooperative learning doesn't end there. Researchers David and Roger Johnson report that

There are over 900 research studies validating the effectiveness of cooperative over competitive and individualistic efforts. This body of research has considerable generalizability since the research has been conducted by many different researchers with markedly different orientations working in different settings and countries and in eleven different decades, since research participants have varied widely as to cultural background, economic class, age, and gender, and since a wide variety of research tasks and measures of the dependent variables have been used. (Johnson & Johnson, 2004)

The sheer breadth of research out there is impressive, to be sure, so it isn't a coincidence that students from all over the United States backed up these strategies as well.

SETTING UP GROUP WORK FOR SUCCESS

Some teachers can be fearful of allowing students to work in groups, but with some frontloading, students can adopt some of the authority in the room through interacting with their peers. Prior to having them work together, it helps to set up different roles to ensure that students are working equitably and that a teacher can also assess students independently. Roles might include the following:

- Recorder
- Reporter
- Timer
- Communications Officer
- Artist

> "Positive effects were found in all major subjects, all grade levels, in urban, rural, and suburban schools, and for high, average, and low achievers."
>
> —David and Roger Johnson

It's also possible to divide up work so that students can choose from a list of artifacts that show collaborative research. For instance, when I run my Superhero PBL unit, the end artifact that the "superhero leagues" must present includes the following:

- A website

- An infographic

- A Public Service announcement

- An Ignite-style slideshow deck to help guide their group oral presentation

  - *Note:* Ignite is like a more efficient and spontaneous TEDTalk. You are only given 20 slides, no more and no less. The slides automatically advance every 15 seconds so there's no time to read. The slides are highly visual and the speaker must be able to speak quickly and efficiently on the topic.

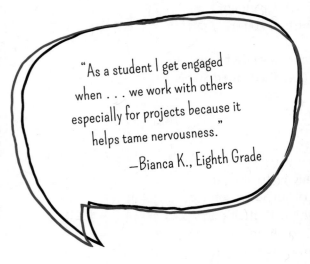

"As a student I get engaged when . . . we work with others especially for projects because it helps tame nervousness."

—Bianca K., Eighth Grade

Although the information in each of these artifacts might include evidence compiled and curated by the whole group, each student is held responsible for one of these assignments.

We see these kinds of roles used often in Writers and Readers workshops, but this is not limited to language arts classes alone. Susie Aames is a seventh-grade math teacher from Los Angeles, CA. She uses collaborative groups daily with her students. This helps not only with academic objectives, but also with classroom management and independent learning. In her lesson about proportional relationships, she groups the kids into the following roles:

- Facilitator

- Harmonizer

- Material Manager

- Resource Manager

She further explains,

> It is within these roles that students are expected to interact with one another and work towards completing the task. Students are put into heterogeneous groups. Students are forced to rely on one another, utilize their notes, and are able to Google. Students were expected to present their findings to the class and any group member would be asked questions and expected to answer them.

Aames then breaks the group goals down into tasks that become an organic way to also differentiate what each group member is responsible to produce. This includes

- construct a data table,
- create a graph of the data,
- write an equation that corresponds with the data in the table and graph, and
- answer the guiding questions.

They also had to collaborate, to bring their contributions to the table by creating a group display.

Aames claims that using collaborative groups in her math class is "effective in engaging students because they are left to their own devices and tools."

By assigning jobs or tasks, teachers can observe students more accurately. Once group work begins, teachers can pay close attention to how students are interacting and assess them on their content knowledge, ability to communicate that content, and collaboration ability.

The students function as pieces of an academic puzzle, each contributing to a greater goal. In fact, The National Education Association (NEA, n.d.) argues, "the most compelling argument for cooperative learning is that it actively engages students in learning. Each student has an opportunity to contribute

"Discussion. My English class is my favorite class because my teacher is totally hands off during discussions. The class becomes entirely student directed . . . I find it liberating and generating ideas myself without being fed by the teacher helps me remember them better."

—Aparna T., Eleventh Grade

in a small group and is more apt to claim ownership of the material."

But one can't merely drop this on the students as a one-and-done scenario. Collaboration and cooperation have to be a paradigm that is adopted early and returned to often.

Think of it this way: Learning is a social activity, and interacting with the material is not meant to only be defined as between a textbook and an individual student. Learning is a joint activity between those in the community. In their ASCD publication, *The New Circles of Learning: Cooperation in the Classroom and School*, David W. Johnson, Roger T. Johnson, and Edythe Johnson Holubec (n.d.) suggest that if teachers are going to establish genuinely cooperative learning, they need to use it for 60% to 80% of the time in their classrooms.

> "Discussions, and learning as a group. Constant solo reading and timed writes makes it really hard to be interested in the class, people tend to be interested more when they see that other people are interested and involved."
>
> —Antony S., Twelfth Grade

It can be scary that first time you dive into the collaborative learning pool. I remember being the teacher with the rows of desks. I remember the first time I shoved those desks around to create a table group. The layout itself was disconcerting, much less the thoughts running through my head:

Would I have control?

How will I manage classroom management?

Will I ever be able to sit down again?

How will I assess who knows what?

How will I learn their names if they aren't facing me the whole time?

Some of these sound silly, I know. But it's where my panicky, lizard brain was at when I first made the shift. When I look back now, it seems ridiculous, because so much has become better and more effective. The answers to the questions, it turned out, were as follows:

Would I have control? Kinda. They ran things better than I could imagine.

How will I manage classroom management? When they are engaged, I didn't have to "sit on" them as much.

Will I ever be able to sit down again? Yep. With them and next to them.

How will I assess who knows what? They are talking more than ever about the content. Just by walking around and keeping my ears open, I learned more than taking only those hands that were raised.

How will I learn their names if they aren't facing me the whole time? You learn by hearing them speak far quicker than by face alone.

But there are strategies you need to put in place when you are asking students to participate in group work. Without them, you're setting up the students and the strategy for failure.

Cornell University's Center for Teaching Excellence developed a short list of ideas to help manage collaborative groups. They are as follows:

- Introduce group work early in the semester to set clear student expectations.

- Plan for each stage of group work.

- Carefully explain to your students how groups will operate and how students will be graded.

- Help students develop the skills they need to succeed in doing group activities, such as using team-building exercises or introducing self-reflection techniques.

- Establish ground rules for participation and contributions.

- Consider using written contracts.

- Incorporate self and peer assessments for group members to evaluate their own and others' contributions. (Center for Teaching Excellence, n.d.)

There is also the strategy of using methods like Socratic Seminar, where civil, evidence-driven group discussion is the focus.

"Grouping students can happen in an infinite number of ways. All mix up the students differently, ask different skills of the students, and ask them to interact with the content through communication with peers."

"About a week ago, Mrs. Harrington did this activity called Socratic Seminar. I think that it was really helpful to me because I got to see what other peers thought about this subject, and not just my opinions. It changed my perspective on the topic."

—Vin Linh V., Seventh Grade

Variations of the open-ended discussion can include developing a fishbowl conversation where a small group models discussion for the larger group. Still another variation builds the fishbowl on representatives that are selected from their own small groups. In other words, the small groups might respond to an open-ended question amongst themselves, then select a representative to carry their message to a panel made up of other group representatives. While speaking to the whole class, a group representative can still solicit advice from other group members in the larger audience. The bottom line is that grouping students can happen in an infinite number of ways. All mix up the students differently, ask different skills of the students, and ask them to interact with the content through communication with peers.

ENGAGE WITH THE CONTENT!

The video to the left opens the window to the classroom of Jason Trapp, high school elective teacher, who is also the focus of this chapter's Engaged Teacher Spotlight. Watch Trapp in action as he sets the task for the students to accomplish collaboratively. As you watch his class and the student interviews, think about the following:

- What tasks does Jason leave open-ended for the students to discover?
- How does he create structure in a collaborative environment?
- What role does group work play in building a classroom community?

Video 1.1 "Let Them Work Together"

COMPETITIVE LEARNING CAN STILL BE COLLABORATIVE LEARNING

A good dose of competition never hurts. It was mentioned often in the survey, and always hand-in-hand with collaboration. This sounds counterintuitive, I know, but when you think about it, there's no reason why these two powerful strategies can't be combined.

Game-based play can generally be used to highlight competition between students, and some mentioned this as a factor in their engagement. However, when side-by-side with collaboration, it couldn't even hold a candle. It just takes targeted merging.

Seth Priebatsch's TEDTalk speech, "The Game Layer on Top of the World" (2010), talks about creating a gaming atmosphere that leverages what the group earns together. This actually leverages a game dynamic known as the communal discovery. In his speech, Priebatsch brings up the need for a shared experience and end goal in how we compete against each other and ourselves and adds that communal discovery is "a dynamic in which everyone has to work together to achieve something. And communal discovery is powerful because it leverages the network that is society to solve problems."

For instance, Free Rice is an online vocabulary game that can be categorized by subject area and levels the questions as it progresses through the game. With each word correctly defined, rice is donated to any number of countries designated by the World Food Programme. By creating something like a thermometer graph in your classroom, you can track the results of the game and the amount of rice earned by the entire classroom community. Thus, a game-based structure, and one that leverages competition, can still help to pull the class together as a collaborative community.

Another example of competitive competition is in an example in my own classroom. The students were already grouped into their "Superhero leagues" (see above). First, I established the goal the groups were competing for. It was for the opportunity to 3D-print their league badges that they had all designed the day before. The reward itself generated some excitement. Then, I introduced the challenge. I was going to read a very complex Jeopardy-esque clue that the group would have to quickly research using Google. The more details that they, as a group, could recall from the sole reading of the clue, the more information they would have to Google to quickly find the correct answer before the other leagues could chime in. I actually filmed some of this in action, and you can view a clip from this activity on the *Just Ask Us* companion site at http://resources.corwin.com/justaskus. Notice their level of engagement as a group. The suspense in my voice doesn't hurt either.

"It's not about creating a clique or a mob, but about creating a family. . . . According to students, this feeling of family engages them as learners."

AN AWESOME BYPRODUCT:
STRONGER CLASSROOM COMMUNITY

There is a huge overlap between the concept of collaboration and that of building community. After all, the foundational blocks of building community is in how we all work together. However, the difference between the two concepts lies in the different ways we as educators seem to address both. And in our student engagement survey, the students tease apart these concepts because they address different needs.

In general, tweens and teens see collaboration in partnerships or in small groups as a way to allow them to talk and debate, to share the workload, and tap into the differences between teammates. Building community, on the other hand, is seen as somehow sharing a universal experience and recognizing the bonding that happens through journeying together as a class.

> "Teamwork assignments help me converse with other students so that we can help each other with specific areas we're not too good with. It's also good, because it helps with social skills."
>
> —Heather T., Tenth Grade

It's about creating a classroom that functions as a cohesive group, one that helps lift each other up through their individual challenges, and models what a riot mentality, one caused by academic achievement, can accomplish. It's not about creating a clique or a mob, but about creating a family.

According to students, this feeling of family engages them as learners. In fact, many said that without a community in the classroom, they couldn't learn. Sure, they could memorize, but they couldn't or wouldn't participate, and we know that deeper learning happens when students interact with each other and with the material. A student who doesn't feel comfortable enough to engage with the classroom isn't going to be engaged with the content either.

In NPR's 2016 segment "How to Fix a Graduation Rate of 1 in 10, Ask the Dropouts," the story approached their clients much like this book does. After asking students why they did not complete their degrees, many were put off by the isolationism of navigating the educational process. In other words, "[t]he dropouts never felt part of the campus community" (Emanuel, 2016).

To combat this, a professor at San Jose State started a group made up of disengaged students, that soon totaled over 300 members, to help build a community of learners that helped each other through their other struggles of life: family, fears of their future, poverty, and so on. As a result, the school had created a program that many students wanted to be a part of. They had created the place to be.

Many times, however, just giving students an opportunity to meet isn't enough. As Sarah Brown Wessing (2012) of the Teaching Channel says, "Other times a group will bond over an experience – a shared victory or a great loss. But most of time, this 'chemistry' isn't handed to us, it's something we have to go out and create."

"Encourage and push people to socialize with their peers so that they look forward to coming to class and working with them. I understand that some students may not get along, well just seperate them or never allow them to sit next to each other, or at least try to go over with them why they do not get along with each other and try to fix the problem."

—Francesco I., Eighth Grade

It takes effort and targeted strategies to develop a deep community in the classroom; but the effort is worth it. The result is not only a classroom that services the social-emotional needs of its students, but it's also one that has the potential for greater academic achievement. After all, "[w]ithout an excellent, intentionally designed, emotional environment (one which builds authentic community in the classroom), the standards and the technologies are of little value," says Anne Shaw (2013) in her post for Edutopia, "Back to School: A Surefire Way for Building Classroom Community."

Of course, our students are the first to recognize the benefits of creating a community in the classroom. It doesn't just create comfort; it triggers achievement as well.

"As middle-school students, we might be tweens or teens who are just starting to find out a way in this large complex world. Our 'teenager-side' might be, at times, very impulsive or emotional. This makes it ever more important for there to be the existence of a classroom community where members support each other. I am most engaged when I feel safe enough to share my ideas and grow in a classroom where I know that my peers and teachers will support me. Teachers, should, in a sense, connect with us and try to create a community between students in the classroom that will support each other. When students don't feel like small individual islands that are put into one classroom, there is less likely to be fear of speaking to the teacher and peers or interacting in classroom activities. As a result, students are more engaged and can learn more from each person in the classroom. Understanding between students and teachers and the formation of a community might be one of the largest contributing factors to student engagement."

—Honor L., Eighth Grade

For many students, it's about the teacher honoring their voices, allowing a give and take of conversation, and modeling how to listen to students so that they may all listen more respectfully to each other.

It's that feeling of contribution that is perhaps key. Even if a student doesn't realize it, the fact that they are heard is what tightens those relationships, both between the teacher and student and between the students themselves.

"I am the most engaged in class when the teacher makes the lesson feels like a conversation instead of a lecture. This encourages me to participate in class and allows me to feel as if I contributed to the discussion."

—Hilary M., Twelfth Grade

"When teachers open up the classroom for free flow of kids opinions I see that kids take the lesson more seriously. Working out of a book or taking notes the whole class while you learn things become boring and it is hard to stay engaged. I think that if a teacher build lets the kids build a community in the classroom the lessons are a lot more fun."

—Anicka P., Seventh Grade

Additionally, many students acknowledge that a sense of community comes from experiencing something together, of taking a shared journey. It's important to note that this can happen in any class, in any subject. For Ethan M., a middle schooler from California, electives are the most engaging lessons because they

> build communities within classrooms. A good example of this would be Spanish. All the students are learning a new language so they can help each other with words or phrases one person is struggling on and eventually they will be able to hold a group conversation in Spanish.

Students also realize how important community is in the world outside of school. Reii R., another California middle schooler, acknowledges that "everyone has a different point of view, mine only being one of them," and asks teachers to help serve to bridge the differences between those points of view.

For many of us, our family is that first group that gives us a sense of community. For those students lucky enough to have that feeling, a classroom or school community extends that circle like a ripple. However, for an unfortunate number of our clients, school may be the first time they might have access to this feeling.

"Because we should learn many things, those things will help us when we go to society. we need comprehensive knowledge and to enrich myself. we are not only learn knowledge also learn how to be a good person. And a student will go to school with teacher and other people. we need learn how to get along with them."

—Katrina L., Twelfth Grade

In a general way, schools try to nurture a feeling of community using mascots and colors to represent the group dynamic. But the real power in building community can be found in our classrooms.

WHAT COLLABORATION LOOKS LIKE IN THE CLASSROOM

It's vital to spend time making students a tight-knit community of learners. It sounds hokey, but it's vital. If you want students to achieve, whether it's at test scores, trophies, or whatever, you can't develop a group that doesn't care about the growth of its individual members. If you want students to improve, you have to have students willing to model for students and students willing to learn from students. This takes building comfort and community. Here are just a few examples of how to do so:

1. **Have the class earn badges and "level up" together.** Use a visual "thermometer" to track the class's growth or accomplishments through a skill. Have the class raise money for a shared cause or collect donations for an agreed-upon charity. Track their advancement toward that goal and celebrate it as a group when that goal is reached.

2. **Honor the diversity in the classroom.** Find ways to incorporate the cultures of your demographics into your content. Bring in related literature or pepper your classroom library with books that have diverse protagonists. Use examples that reference different geographical locations or traditions.

3. **Have students contribute to shared documents as often as possible.** Not only does this grant transparency to the thought process of higher-level students, but it also eventually contributes to the community feel of a classroom. The purpose of the shared document can also focus on building community itself. For instance, within the first two days of class, I create a shared document called a "Classroom Constitution" (Figures 1.1 and 1.2). The students all add goals for the classroom regarding behavior, academic standards, peer relations, and so on. This document then gets printed out, and each student signs it as a promise to how we will function together. It also gets posted onto our classroom website.

> "What engages me as a student is when I'm learning about my culture it really interest me because I feel like I'm a part of the conversation."
>
> —Claire G., Seventh Grade

4. **Decide that no matter what quality is submitted, all students must participate in the "fun" culminating activity.** Case in point, I used to be the coach of a very successful and very large middle school speech and debate team. I would have coaches come and observe me occasionally because they wanted to know how my team, a diverse group of students from a Title I district,

FIGURE 1.1

CLASSROOM CONSTITUTION

Photo courtesy of Heather Wolpert-Gawron

FIGURE 1.2

CLASSROOM CONSTITUTION

We vow to joust with our own thought to make them stronger and more developed.
We vow to listen to each other no matter how different our opinions are
Thou shall vow to spread thine wings and fly over the Sea of Problems.
Those in Room 1 shall always be truthful and loyal, not only to their fellow acquaintances, but also to people outside of the classroom, with fair and equal treatment..
Those who call themselves the learners of Room 1 will realize that learning is not a task, requirement, or chore, but a choice that we all have to consciously make.
Those in Room 1 shall embrace the wackiest of ideas because no idea is a "bad" idea sometimes the "bad" idea could be the most incredible one
We vow to not let the fear of failure or rejection stop us from achieving our goals and reaching our full potential as academic scholars
We solemnly swear to work with one another no matter what sexuality, gender, race or religion the other person is.
Thou shalt not be afraid of criticism, criticism is what builds us internally and fills us with knowledge and ideas
We vow to face our errors and mistakes not with denial and excuses, but with an open mind.
Those in Room 1 shall try hard and exceed classroom expectations.
Thou shalt not fight with each other
One shall exceed the limits, stopping at nothing to get to their goal.
Thou shall exceed thine expectations of others and soar above and beyond.
We vow to aspire for knowledge, and never give up.
Thou shalt not look upon failure with negativity and sorrow, but rather with joy and thankfulness, for it will make you more successful in the future.
Those in Room 1 shall constantly aspire to acquire new knowledge and continue to augment their writing skills.
Thou shall hold truth in all situations, for blasphemy unto others harms much more than the cold truth.
We vow to always put our best effort into the work we produce for final products that we are proud of.
We vow to respect boundaries.
Thou shalt not consume food within Room 1, if you do, be vigilant
Thou shall not give into peer pressure, but make thine own decisions
Those in Room 1 shall work together as one to create the best work we can make
Thou shalt not deceive or use trickery upon fellow classmates; the concept of toleration shall be used to every single person.
Those in Room 1 shall be creative and original without the influence of others.
Thou shall not give in to stupidity, but rather be the SmartWater that douses the flame.
Those in Room 1 shall be able to listen to music during class time.
We vow to be internet safe and not go onto irrelevant websites

could achieve as well as we did. The secret sauce was simple: We built community.

One of the ways was to insist that the whole team went to competitions together. The EL students, the honors kids, the SPED kids, and so on, they all had to attend the tournaments, on the buses, and compete whether their speeches were high quality or not. Why? It wasn't to torture those who would never trophy. It was because when we returned on those buses, the singing and applauding were bonding. They all shared the experience of the event, as a team, and came out the other end, together.

5. **Create group activities that constantly shuffle kids around.** Desegregate the class immediately; break down cliques and self-imposed groupings so that the clique is the classroom community itself.

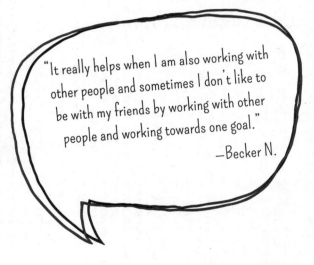

"It really helps when I am also working with other people and sometimes I don't like to be with my friends by working with other people and working towards one goal."

—Becker N.

For instance, one activity I've done is have students perform lip-sync music videos, with the sole purpose of building community. Right at the onset, I make sure I group students diversely as much as possible: different ability levels, different grade levels, different races, different levels of friendships, different elementary schools (regions of the city), and so forth. I break up any group that came into the door together. Students are then given the task to find a 2-minute song and record a lip-sync to that song—the goofier the better. It's about leaving all dignity at the door, working together, and getting to know others. Then, we have a film festival.

Create heterogeneous groups, ones that aren't formed up of kids of similar levels. Many times, grouping by level allows for targeted guidance. But when it comes to building community, shake 'em up like Chex Party Mix.

The common element in many of this chapter's activities is, of course, collaboration. It's cyclical, you see. Collaboration leads to community, and a deeper community leads to greater student engagement.

It comes from a very targeted way of teaching the concept of "team," and to quote the Bard, it's a very Henry V way of thinking:

> "For he who sheds his blood with me today shall be my brother."

Cultivate that way of thinking and you will have developed a community of those who love learning together. Be it for a math Olympiad, a chess club, a language arts class, or a speech and debate team, working together to learn the love of learning is what school should be about.

ENGAGE WITH THE CONTENT!

The video featured here dives further into how Mr. Trapp's lesson not only uses collaboration, but also builds community in the process, specifically by building a classroom brand. In the "Engaging Teacher Spotlight" lesson below, Jason shares more about how to build a brand in order to find symbolic cohesion as a classroom community.

As you watch the video, notice the following:

- How are students interacting and sharing ideas about the job at hand?
- What are skills that the students are learning in building a classroom brand that might help them outside of school?
- How might a classroom brand be used throughout the school year to continuously maintain community?

Video 1.2 Building a Community Through a Brand

ENGAGING TEACHER SPOTLIGHT

Here is one lesson from high school electives teacher Jason Trapp, whom we met in Video 1.2. Jason has had a varied career in both elementary and secondary schools. Additionally, he worked with children during his deployment in Afghanistan as well. Below is just one of his lessons that he uses to build community in his clubs and elective classes. In it, he guides his students to create a brand for their classroom, a powerful symbol of their collaborative community.

REINFORCE COMMUNITY WITH A CLASSROOM BRAND

Band geeks, slackers, speech kids, jocks, thespians, ASB royalty, cool kids, and the like. Each of these adolescent students walks into your classroom and even though they appear to be unique individuals, they all share one identity in common: regardless of age or grade, they are all consumers. Whether they are fourth graders, middle schoolers, or juniors in high school, they are all searching for the same commodity: identity. The community you build can offer students that identity; the brand you cultivate can reinforce the other unifying classroom management practices you currently have in place to build an inclusive community. Building a strong brand for your class will help students identify and connect with their classmates even if they have nothing else in common other than the fact that they have the same fourth-period elective with you as their teacher.

Close your eyes and visualize a Nike T-shirt, a Snickers wrapper, or yearbook. The *Swoosh*. Helvetica. Every successful brand reinforces identity through four cohesive elements: a logo, font choice, tagline, and color palette. These elements work in concert to sell consumers a product. By cultivating a strong brand for your classroom, you will reinforce a community for your students to buy into.

SO WHAT ARE THE STEPS TO CREATING A CLASSROOM BRAND?

1. **Come up with a name**. It might be based on your name: *Cabrera, Inc.* It might be based on your school's mascot or room number: *Room 11 Tribe*. It might be based on the class you teach or the club you advise: In the case of the lesson I am relating here for my Gabrielino high school yearbook elective, we used *GHS Ash-a-Wut YBK. GHS is named for the Gabrielino tribe that inhabited the area around the San Gabriel Mission. Gabrielino is the name the Spanish missionaries gave the tribe. The tribe called themselves Tongva. Ash-a-Wut means "eagle" in the Tongva dialect.*

2. **Look for inspiration**. Go to the sources your students streetwear lookbooks; college recruiting materials, or even better, college identity guides; or your own school's mascot or athletic uniforms. Look at all the elements, but especially typography and font choice. These materials are designed to

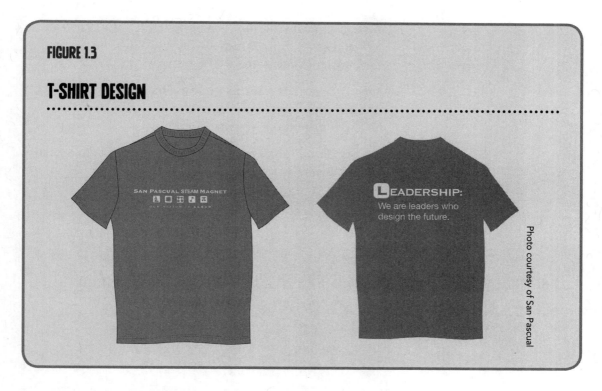

FIGURE 1.3

T-SHIRT DESIGN

SAN PASCUAL STEAM MAGNET

LEADERSHIP:
We are leaders who
design the future.

Photo courtesy of San Pascual

hook your students' attention. If you "borrow" some of their elements your brand will enjoy the same success.

For example, see the 2014 GHS Ash-a-Wut YBK yearbook, *It Starts With YOU*. The t-shirt we sold to the student body (Figure 1.4) featured design elements from the book and our school's signature palm trees. Consider two popular streetwear designs from HUF and Diamond Supply Co. We leveraged what was popular among the student body to sell our book, reinforce our class's own brand, and recruit new students to the staff. We became the intersection of school and cool as the "it" class on campus.

3. **Build Version A of your logo**. First, choose a font—or two. You can say a lot just by the way your font looks. Different fonts convey different feelings. When Lebron James first left Cleveland for Miami, Cavaliers owner Dan Gilbert wrote a scathing letter directed at the King, except it was printed in Comic Sans and lost all its teeth. Third, add a visual element—hipster lines, crossed arrows, a ribbon? Last, work on a color palette: Bold? Pastels? Ombre?

4. **Create two more full versions.** Ensure that each version includes all visual design elements with slight variations.

Version A: Sans serif font heavy and light. Version B: Slab serif and script font. Version C: Helvetica. Just no Comic Sans. Never Comic Sans.

5. **Run it through a focus group.** Share it with your niece in eighth grade, students who just graduated, your neighbor's son too. Get some opinions.

6. **Go big.** Posters, t-shirts, class Twitter, letterhead, Snapchat filters if you're a club.

WHAT ARE SOME TOOLS I CAN USE?

Adobe Creative Cloud: The design industry standard is Adobe Creative Cloud. Between InDesign, Photoshop, and Illustrator, you can design down to the pica (one-sixth of an inch). However, even the educator pricing of $19.99/month is probably cost prohibitive for most.

Pages: Another option for Mac users. Better than Word.

Canva: Free and web based. Has preloaded font combinations and design templates, but you can also create your own. Different sized canvases for social media uses are offered as well.

Adobe Color: Not too confident with combining complementary or analogous colors? Look no further. Will also give you RGB and HEX color codes.

Reinforcing your community by cultivating a strong classroom brand will help students connect with their classmates and feel a sense of identity in your room.

DISCUSSION QUESTIONS

1. How might you support students building their own Personal Learning Communities in your own classroom?

2. What are the various ways you can have students work together yet assess them independently?

3. When might it be advantageous to assign students to specific groups and allow for student choice? How might you combine both strategies?

4. Think of your favorite, albeit more traditionally crafted, lesson. How might you modify this beloved lesson to include small-group collaboration?

Photo courtesy of Davis Lester

CHAPTER TWO

MAKE LEARNING MORE VISUAL AND UTILIZE TECHNOLOGY

"Help me visualize it more clearly."

OVERVIEW

When we talk about a successful learning strategy, we want one that helps content to stick. We want to find methods of delivery that help information to enter the brain and remain there to be processed and chewed on, mulled over, and retained.

One of the most engaging methods of learning that came up over and over in our student survey was that of teaching with visuals. An offshoot of that was the use of technology. Based on students' responses, using visuals appeared as a macro concept, while using technology was a micro concept that consistently helped deliver the visuals to the students.

> "I learn better when I see something. That is the best way I have been able to learn easily that also stick to me. It has to be interactive, colorful, and have a wow factor to keep me engaged in the activity."
>
> —Benjamin A., Tenth Grade

In other words, many times within the same response, students would state that they needed visuals, then zoom in to an example that utilized technology as a means to introduce that visual to the learners. For that reason, I have combined these two concepts together in this one chapter.

"[U]sing visuals appeared as a macro concept, while using technology was a micro concept that consistently helped deliver the visuals to the students."

Visual supports are not only engaging; they are vital in how students, actually all people, process information. While this book is from the point of view of Grade 6–12 students, we know that using visuals even helps those in higher education to learn more deeply.

In fact, a recent study by Mark A. McDaniel, a professor of psychology at Washington University in St. Louis, and graduate student Dung C. Bui, found that

> college students who had visual aids given to them before a science lecture were better able to understand and remember the lecture . . . illustrative diagrams helped more than outlines. . . . Participants given illustrative diagrams likely engaged in deeper levels of processing while listening to the lecture. (McDaniel, 2015)

"Visuals make abstract learning more concrete."

We use visuals because they can be a universal part of our communication system that helps students express themselves.

They can attract attention to the important elements of a concept. They can help reduce student anxiety, in particular when faced with a wall of text or speech. They can create an environment more conducive to community and comfort. Visuals make abstract learning more concrete.

In addition, using visuals helps trigger our brains in ways that cannot be seen to the naked eye.

Studies show the following:

- Visuals can help information stick to long-term memory and increase retention.

- Visuals can be interpreted faster than speech alone.

- Visuals can activate emotions and feelings far more quickly and with greater force.

In Stanford University's white paper, "Visual Language and Converging Technologies in the Next 10–15 Years (and Beyond)," author Robert E. Horn, explains that

> [w]hen words and visual elements are closely entwined, we create something new and we augment our communal intelligence. . . . Visual language has the potential for increasing "human bandwidth"—the capacity to take in, comprehend, and more efficiently synthesize large amounts of new information. (Horn, n.d.)

This concept of increasing "human bandwidth" is a great—for lack of a better word—*visual* of what happens when to our brains when visuals are used in teaching practice.

THIS IS OUR BRAIN ON VISUALS

When we talk about how our brains learn, that is, how brains absorb information, store it, and categorize it, we are talking about the concept of encoding.

"I enjoy when . . . the teacher works some sort of artistic, creative component into the lesson. This forces me to think about the topic and how to represent it, and generally increases my understanding."

—Iris D., Seventh Grade

"[V]isual language has the potential for increasing 'human bandwidth'— the capacity to take in, comprehend, and more efficiently synthesize large amounts of new information."

—Robert E. Horn

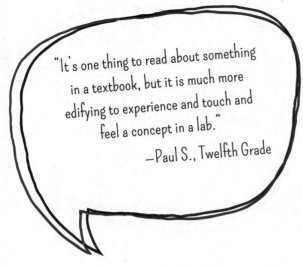

"It's one thing to read about something in a textbook, but it is much more edifying to experience and touch and feel a concept in a lab."

—Paul S., Twelfth Grade

Say a student hears the fact that China's Zhou Dynasty lasted from 1046 to 256 BC, and then, 4 days later, that same student is asked to recall that fact. If that student can't somehow retrieve that memory, it's possible that it was never encoded properly in the first place. That is, it never made it into their memory banks at all.

If you think of your brain like a computer, encoding is like clicking "save." Encoding happens when connections with the brain cells, the neurons, are formed. It's like they form little pathways between them that act to conduct the information around the brain. When a person experiences something or learns something, the brain creates pathways to store the information in its memory banks.

Once you encode something, you should be able to recall it from short- or long-term memory.

Basically, it works like this:

Fact > A sense(s) is triggered. > Fact enters brain. > Signal is sent to the thalamus for processing. > The hippocampus picks it up and decides if it should be sent to long-term memory.

So how does the hippocampus decide what gets sent there?

The answer is that it kinda, sorta, in a way, asks for advice from another location in the brain.

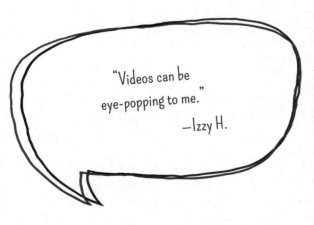

"Videos can be eye-popping to me."

—Izzy H.

Encoding visuals is related to the amygdala, which is close to the hippocampus. The amygdala is the place in charge of assigning and feeling emotions. Visuals, therefore, cannot only trigger greater comprehension, but emotions as well. As such, immediate connections of possibly greater varieties are made, enabling the hippocampus to make its decision.

Hippocampus:	Hey, this piece of information just arrived! Where do I put this thing?
Amygdala:	What's been triggered? How does it make you feel?
Hippocampus:	Well, there's this caption, some words here, something about the War of 1812. Blah-blah-blah.
Amygdala:	You're not giving me a lot to go on here. Anything else?
Hippocampus:	Well, it's got this picture too. I think I'm feeling something looking at this thing. This guy's in chains and the old guns are pointed at him. There's this woman crying, and there are ships in the background. I think I've seen those ships before, in a movie. If I click on the picture, there's a pop-up that links to a gallery of other images from the war.
Amygdala:	Sounds worthy of long-term memory to me. You've got more to mull over about it. Put it over there (points to the long-term memory banks).

Make sure that multiple senses, in particular visuals, are triggered in a lesson. That way, information is ushered into the brain and is more likely encoded into long-term memory banks.

There are arguably three main ways in which information can be encoded:

1. Acoustic—through sound

2. Semantic—through the meaning of things and how we connect to the material

3. Visual—through viewing pictures, images, icons, videos, and so on, and creating mental images that can then be processed and stored

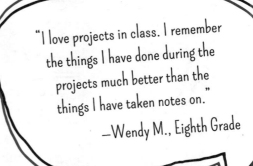

"I love projects in class. I remember the things I have done during the projects much better than the things I have taken notes on."

—Wendy M., Eighth Grade

Now, while all three of these can be delivered easily through technology, there is a hierarchy that helps us determine which strategy to invest in when we can.

While evidence shows that acoustic coding is the primary system that stores information into short-term memory, the fact is that research tells us that if long-term memory is our goal, using visuals is the way to go.

According to *Psychology Today*'s Dr. Haig Kouyoumdjian (2012),

A large body of research indicates that visual cues help us to better retrieve and remember information. The research outcomes on visual learning make complete sense when you consider that our *brain* is mainly an image processor (much of our sensory cortex is devoted to vision), not a word processor. . . . There are countless studies that have confirmed the power of visual imagery in learning. For instance, one study asked students to remember many groups of three words each, such as dog, bike, and street. Students who tried to remember the words by repeating them over and over again did poorly on recall. In comparison, students who made the effort to make visual associations with the three words, such as imagining a dog riding a bike down the street, had significantly better recall.

> "As a student, I believe that video teachers show us make us engage in class. The information that I obtain form the video help me make a connection with the lecture the teachers provided. For example, in AP Language & Composition, we watch Hamlet movie as we read through the book. This helped me understand the book better and get involved in class discussion."
>
> —Hae-seong S., Senior

Additionally, Edgar Dale wrote that by listening to a lecture alone, students could recall only 25% of what was said and only 10%–20% after 3 days had passed.

If information is read, 72% of information can be recalled after 3 hours, but this percentage drops to only 10% after 3 days.

However, if visual and verbal systems are stimulated, say in an illustrated lecture, 80% of information can be recalled after 3 hours and 65% can still be recalled after 3 days (Dale, 1969). Nevertheless, according to a 2009 study by the University of Illinois, despite the fact that only 10% of secondary learners are designated as auditory learners, over 80% of information is still delivered orally. This is made further frustrating by the fact that over 65% of the population is thought to be visual learners. There is further evidence that proves that the brain processes visuals over 60,000 times faster than mere text.

Furthermore, neurologists have found that the brain "can identify images seen for as little as 13 milliseconds" (Visual Teaching Alliance, n.d.).

"The thing that engages me the most in class is when teachers show examples such as when we learn about volcanoes and the teachers brings in a model volcano that we can examine. That helps me visualize more clearly than by just reading a description off a book. . . . What also helps would be if a teacher had a fun classroom because nobody likes sitting in a room that is plain with not even a picture on the wall. I know that too many things can lead to distractions but if the things around the classroom are educational, students might just be a bit curious and would like to learn more about what all the object and posters mean."

—Tracy M., Seventh Grade

Did you glaze over while reading all those statistics? Try looking at them using the student-created infographic below.

USING VISUALS IN THE CLASSROOM BY ARLENE C

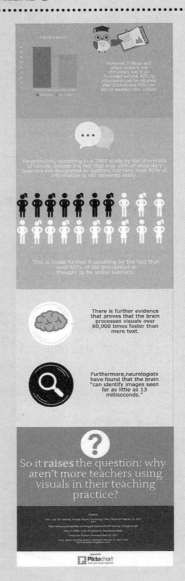

So it raises the question: Why aren't more teachers using visuals in their teaching practice?

LEARNING THROUGH VISUALS

It's possible that many teachers themselves fall more into the 10% of auditory learners and so don't inherently develop or implement as many visual-based lessons.

So it's not hard to believe that students are longing for more visuals and recognize that this strategy is effective. The research from educational experts states it, and the students themselves know it to be true as well. Using visuals isn't just about making lessons more stimulating; they actually give access to learning where previously, sans visuals, there was little to none.

We've all seen the charts or seen a slide with the following (or something like it):

1% of what is learned is from the sense of TASTE;

1.5% of what is learned is from the sense of TOUCH;

3.5% of what is learned is from the logic of SMELL;

11% of what is educated is from the logic of HEARING; and

83% of what is learned is from the sense of SIGHT.

And I have to say, it's easy to find visual-based tools that can enhance any subject-area lesson. Teachers can use the following visuals:

- Images
- Timelines
- Concept Maps

"I like it when teachers draw pictures on the boards."
—Bella R., Senior

"I become engages as a student when there are plenty of visuals such as films, animations, etc. . . . I am engaged when entertained with learning."
—Brook R., Tenth Grade

"[T]o see how to do it. like in pictures or graphs to see how to do it not just in words."
—Kathy B., Seventh Grade

> "Mr. Tang teaches math lessons very well . . . when he teaches, he draws pictures, uses videos, and even uses a few 'gaming' websites (of course educational related) and makes it better to comprehend."
>
> —Wiltur C.

> "Technology! I am such a tech enthusiast and love using modern means of learning instead of just a number two pencil and a sheet of college ruled paper."
>
> —Noah, Middle School

- Charts/Graphs
- Videos
- Infographics
- Symbols
- Realia
- Labs

So how does an educator include visuals, videos, infographics, and symbols into text? How does a teacher stimulate multiple senses at once in order to both engage students and possibly see more information get stored in long-term memory?

The answer rests in the arms of technology.

Technology can be a vehicle for many different kinds of visuals, from images to videos, and even grants students the ability to interact with text in a more engaging way. For this reason, I want to go a little deeper into technology as an offshoot of the visual concept before rounding it all up into some end-of-chapter advice on how to integrate visuals (including technology) into the classroom.

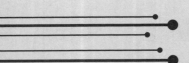

ENGAGE WITH THE CONTENT

In this video, we introduce you to Liz Harrington's ELA seventh-grade classroom where she uses visuals to enhance comprehension and engagement during a performance-based assessment. You'll also hear from Liz herself, her students, and other teachers about how visuals are necessary to teach any subject. As you watch, think about the following:

Video 2.1 Use Visuals to Engage Learners

- How does the use of visuals help communicate the content?
- How does the use the visuals aid in the rigor of the assessment?
- What are the different kinds of visuals that can be used to enhance your own subject area?

THE ONE VISUAL TOOL TO RULE THEM ALL: TECHNOLOGY

The use of technology came up with almost the same frequency as the broader, though related topic of using visuals in general. And of those responses, many students mentioned that it was the technology itself that enabled them to have access to the visuals that they found so engaging.

Oftentimes, when students brought up technology, they stressed that in addition to giving them more access to visual resources and tools, technology also

- Allowed them to be more independent in their learning
- Helped them be more comfortable within the classroom
- Prepared them better for the futures they might face after school

"I like when teachers use technology in our lesson plans because its something we know how to use and it will make it more understandable . . . lessons that use [it] have lots of color and visuals."

—Shakira G., Tenth Grade

"One thing I love in math is the activities, like making a wordle . . . and I want to learn as much information as I can about technology."

—Connor C.

Note: A Word Cloud is a visualization of text formed into a "cloud" by a program such as Wordle or Taxedo. Many times, the most frequent word in the passage appears larger and can, at times, indicate main idea.

(Continued)

(Continued)

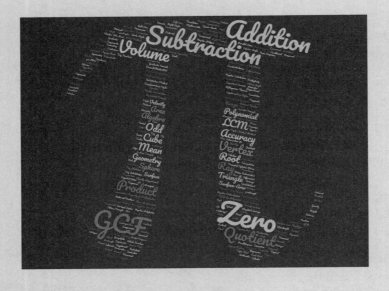

Technology brings games easily into the classroom:
"I like when we use technology to engage us in lessons such as play Ancient Greece Jeopardy. I also like when we do Kahoot lessons because it makes doing math more fun."

—Alon

"Lessons involving technology or some sort of 'game' helps me, as well as videos or diagrams."

—Emily C., Twelfth Grade, Munising, Michigan

Then there were those who loved how technology allowed them to play educational games like Kahoot where students could compete against their peers to answer questions developed by the teacher. Using Kahoot, students can also then see how their responses stacked up against others.

The ease of which technology can help teachers embed a whole array of visuals is staggering. Here is just one account from an English language teacher in Colorado:

Technology use is an intrinsic part of Alma's classroom; in fact, her class takes place in a computer lab. By using visual supports (clip art and other graphic images), the students are able to see an object and associate it with the words they see and hear. She uses Power Point presentations in her lectures to introduce colors, geography concepts, and an array of nouns. She finds this method especially important for visual learners and those students with low literacy levels. Through visual representations, she helps her students build the vocabulary needed for the content lessons in their regular classes (she is required to teach some of this content in the ESL class). . . . Because she wants her students to be self-learners, the Internet plays an important role in her classroom. Often she will create a list of sites with useful information (and very importantly, at an adequate reading level!), then ask her students to create a presentation based on research through those sites. She often has her students use webs or concept maps to organize the information from their searches. ("Using Technology to Create a Visual Learning Environment," n.d.).

And it isn't just about the presentation of material that makes technology so accessible. We aren't just talking about how students consume material. We are also talking about the ease of creating as well.

Blogger Kris Schrotenboer wrote a piece in the EmergingEdTech blog that spoke of her observations along these lines:

"These days, students are experts with technology. They know keyboard shortcuts, the best websites for definitions, possibly everything. In addition, when students get the chance to have a laptop on their desk . . . they feel important. They feel great, that they get the chance to participate in an activity where the teacher trusts them with the laptop."

—Katie L.

Since implementing visual technology within my classroom, I have individualized my instruction based on both student needs and curriculum demands. As a result, my students' comprehension of course material has improved drastically and I am now able to present information in a multitude of ways. Furthermore, by presenting short bites of visual information that correlate to assigned tasks, the acquisition of knowledge is immediately followed by the application of skill. (Schrotenboer, 2014)

"I want to learn all the important bells and whistles of how to use a computer."

—Logan, Sixth Grade

"One of the things that engages me are online discussions. They require no talking at all and also no distractions."

—Curtis C.

Technology allows teachers to continue following best practices of pacing, providing access to information, stimulating multiple senses, and developing the skills needed for their future.

In other words, you don't have to make massive changes to add layers of technology to your successfully paced lessons. In fact, I would argue that technology makes lessons more efficient.

Let's say, in a nontechnological environment, you utilize the following method of daily pacing:

1. Start with an introduction activity

2. Continue with a mini-lesson

3. Model

4. Release them to do small group work and/or an individual activity

5. Exit card/Informal assessment

However, you can keep the same pacing and elements while integrating more visually stimulating strategies using technology. It might look like the following:

1. Share a screencast with your students that they can watch the night before. This screencast could introduce them to a concept.

2. When the students come to class the next day, have them research a new resource on the concept using Junior Google or Instagrok and add it to a Google Form.

3. Once the spreadsheet from the Google Form is created, share it with the class via Google Classroom.

4. In small groups, have the students create collaborative hyperdocs of student-selected resources made up of the vetted links on the sheet. Have them chunk the resources in a more visual way using subheadings, bullets, and numbering.

They can also add images that symbolize the resource as well.

5. As an exit card, have the students answer an essential question by creating their own 30-second screencast that they share with you via email or Google Classroom.

"I also like using all the technology like laptops and stuff. For some reason, when it comes to crafts or graphic stuff, I get totally involved and kind of like morphed into my own little world of designing."

—Madison S.

The technology used in the above scenario reflects a more visual way students can research, organize, curate, and communicate. The technology allows students to view resources using more visual search engines like Junior Google, which uses pictures next to each Google Entry, and Instagrok, which uses a Web rather than a list to help display search hits. The technology allowed students to categorize the reference materials they found by first viewing it on a spreadsheet as a whole class and then chunking the resources onto a hyperdoc. In the above scenario, by asking students to categorize the resources using subheadings, bullets, and numbering, we are helping them embed the student-created resource into their brain in a more visual way.

A *hyperdoc* is a document (or slideshow) that is peppered with live links to allow the reader to interact with the text more deeply. A hyperdoc might include the following:

- Links to explore various research on a topic. One link might bring the student to a video. Another might lead the student to an image or article.
- Links leading students to a choice of graphic organizers
- Links to activities to apply what students have learned
- Links to assessments and other formal and informal methods of evaluation

Hyperdocs are another way technology can be used as a more engaging vehicle for lesson structure.

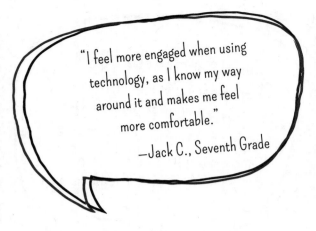

"I feel more engaged when using technology, as I know my way around it and makes me feel more comfortable."

—Jack C., Seventh Grade

Finally, the technology gives students quick and easy access to both a camera (to film themselves answering a brief question) as well as to a publishing workflow (to send their responses to their audience, in this case, their teacher).

The visuals, as well as the tools that permit the visuals to happen so easily, engage the students to encourage more independent learning.

In an interview with Sheryl Nussbaum-Beach, the co-founder and chief executive officer of Powerful Learning Practice as well as an advisor to the U.S. Department of Education's Connected Educators Initiative, she stressed that

> [g]reat technology use challenges kids to learn through active involvement. . . . I guess if I was going to put it in a nutshell, best uses of technology in a classroom are uses that honor the learner, protect student agency, and support deep, meaningful exploration of content. Students should be using the technology to produce knowledge and to show mastery and understanding of learning—not just consuming content with it. . . . [T]echnology allows us to connect with people around the world with a few clicks of a button, graph in seconds what once took hours to do, and learn anything, anytime, anywhere we are motivated to do so—makes it an incredibly powerful draw. Technology is a nimble tool for knowledge production. It is a brilliant canvas across which we can stroke our most beautiful creations. It enables us to do things faster, smarter and make connections and comparisons that once were impossible. I mean seriously, what's to not like? Who wouldn't be attracted? (Nussbaum-Beach, 2016)

"Computer helps me stay on track."

—Elijiah

In other words, technology allows teachers to employ great practices and keep up with the accelerated pacing in today's educational world that demands we teach both content and skills.

Nussbaum-Beach also listed a number of possible ways to use technology. She says kids using technology correctly in school are engaged in the following ways:

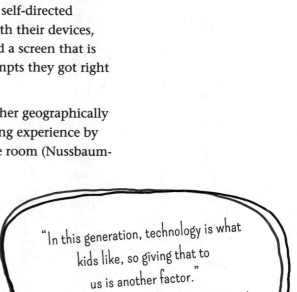

"[W]hen I get older, I know that technology is going to play a major role for my future."

—Jessica T., Tenth Grade

- Up moving, snapping pictures, doing a video-based interview

- Recording an experiment or finding a "just in time" answer to a question raised in a collaborative team meeting about a group project

- Learning through problem finding and self-directed experimentation with trial and error with their devices, rather than endless hours sitting behind a screen that is adaptively tracking the number of attempts they got right and wrong

- Accessing subject matter experts and other geographically diverse students to be part of the learning experience by streaming them and their ideas into the room (Nussbaum-Beach, 2016)

She acknowledges that technology must be combined with good practice. After all, studies are showing that technology use releases dopamine, the chemical in the brain associated with pleasure. In the extreme, it can lead to addiction, but when used correctly, technology in the classroom leads to engagement.

"In this generation, technology is what kids like, so giving that to us is another factor."

—Georgia, Middle School

Utilizing technology is vital in making our lessons more visual. They make implementation easier, more multi-modal, and engaging. Making our lessons more engaging using visuals is how we guide students to both more deeply consume information as well as more deeply create it.

WHAT USING MORE VISUALS (AND TECHNOLOGY) LOOKS LIKE IN THE CLASSROOM

While this chapter has included general suggestions already about ways to use visuals in the classroom, I wanted to get more specific about possible implementation. Here is a list of different strategies you can use, both technological and offline, to more easily incorporate visuals in our practice:

1. **Include realia in your lessons.** Another word for *realia* could be *props*. In other words, bring in actual items to help kids visualize a concept. Realia makes abstract concepts more concrete. For instance, when I teach sensory details in writing, I bring in disinfecting wipes. I ask the students to use similes to describe them based on their senses:

What does this smell like? I generally get comments about lemons.

When you smell it, what happens to your tongue? In other words, what does it taste like? I get comments like bitter and bright.

What does it look like? If a student looks closely, the wipes are perforated like a quilt.

What does it sound like? I hit the side of the canister and snap the lid shut with a click.

What does it make you feel like? I tell them that this smell of clean always brings me back to summer camp and the locker rooms before swimming.

Another example of realia that I use is in my classroom library. I have little items and dolls that represent different genres all throughout the shelves. I have the bust of Sherlock Holmes in front of my mystery section. I have a UFO in my sci-fi section. I have the head of pirate Capt. Morgan leaning by my historical fiction section.

"In science, we do a flipped classroom which gives us more time to do worksheets and labs during class with the help of the teacher."

—Kayla B., Sixth Grade

2. **Use manipulatives for them to use with their hands.** An offshoot of realia are manipulatives, those hands-on objects that kids can handle in order to fully understand a concept. You might find these in math like when students use decimal cubes or create geometric shapes using rubber bands.

3. **Teach students how to write using a variety of text structures.** Text structures are also a visual way to break up thoughts and organize them differently, and word processing allows a student to use different text structures very easily. Have students go back through their notes and insert different structures as a reflection activity. Have them create a professional-looking newspaper or magazine on any topic. Have them break up their essays using any of the following or more:

   Bold

   Subheadings of different sizes

   Variety in fonts

   Numbering

   Bullets

4. **Vocabulary Posters.** Have students visualize any content area vocabulary by creating posters that are divided up into quadrants. In one square, the student writes the word. In the next, the student writes the definition. In the third, the student writes it in a sentence, and in the last square, the student draws a picture that helps to see the vocabulary in action. It can be a symbolic or a literal interpretation of the word. See Figure 2.1.

5. **Develop hyperdocs to deliver multimedia information.** While I have defined hyperdocs above, I wanted to stress that they really are ideal for delivering multimedia information. Images can easily be coupled with text, videos, or charts to further illuminate the concept, and activities can be weaved throughout the resources.

6. **Use slides to help chunk information.** More text-heavy information can be easily broken up using slides. Whether you use Google Slideshow, PowerPoint,

FIGURE 2.1

A VOCABULARY POSTER OF THE WORD *PROPORTION*

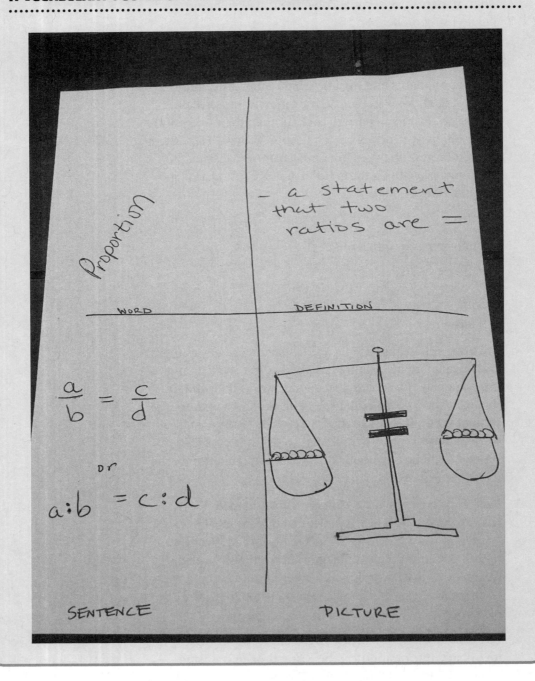

Mac Keynote, and so on. slides can allow a student or teacher to organize by pages. The pages can reflect different ways to organize essays or concepts. For instance, in a literary analysis, a student can chunk his essay by dividing it up on slides called Introduction, Evidence, and Commentary. In science, a student can chunk her writing by breaking the slides up by the scientific method: Question, Research, Hypothesis, Observations, Analysis, Report. And, of course, as always, include images on every slide. *Note*: Remind students that if they don't own the image, they have to cite each one they find!

7. **Have students develop digital textbooks of their own.** Programs like iBooks allow students to create their own textbooks, embedding images that support the content, whatever they may be. For instance, say a student creates their own math textbook. On one page may be the definition of a term, but it might also be accompanied by a diagram. There might also by an equation that is explained by a video of the student who recorded a screencast to justify the outcome. If you don't have Apple products in your classrooms or labs, however, you can still create "textbooks" by building them on Slideshows in Google, or on a program like PowerPoint. *Note:* If your school is considering adopting a digital textbook for your subject, many from different companies not only read the text to you, but can also highlight the text in real time to align with what's being read. This helps those who need more visuals when you are teaching literacy, like English language learners and special education students.

8. **Use graphs and motion charts.** We know that graphs like bar graphs and pie charts are wonderful ways to help visualize data. However, did you know that Google Motion Charts actually animate data that change over time? You can see an example of this in Hanz Rosling's TEDTalk

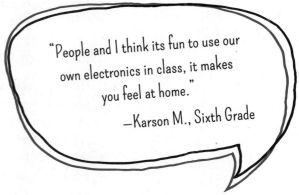

"People and I think its fun to use our own electronics in class, it makes you feel at home."

—Karson M., Sixth Grade

called "The Best Stats You've Ever Seen." He also highlights this kind of technology in his BBC Four's "200 Countries, 200 Years, 4 Minutes—The Joy of Stats" available at www.youtube.com/watch?v=jbkSRLYSojo.

9. **Show videos.** Of course, you can use all kinds of videos to help illustrate a concept, but some are better than others. TEDTalks (mentioned previously in this chapter), for instance, aren't just videos. They are interactive visual and audio experiences. While watching the video, one can view the transcripts as they highlight automatically during the performance. Again, technology allows a multimedia experience to engage multiple senses.

10. **Create screencasts**. Screencasts are short, easy-to-produce videos using the camera on one's computer. It allows a teacher or student to not only film their face, but also to capture on video what they are doing on their own monitor. A teacher can produce one as a mini-lesson so students can view them on their own time to either frontload or review a concept. A student can produce one as an informal assessment communicating what they know. Screencasts allow for individualized learning and assessing in a more visual way. You can use one of the following programs:

    Screencastify—free as a Google Chrome Extension

    Screencastomatic—free and Web based

    Screenflow—paid program but user-friendly

    I have included two Screencasting examples on the companion website for this book. One is of me giving feedback to a student on his writing quality. The other is of a student's "Book Talk," an alternative to your run-of-the-mill book report. Check out http://resources.corwin.com/justaskus to watch these screencasts.

11. **Go on a virtual field trip.** Technology grants classrooms access to museums, theaters, libraries, and events all over the world. Rather than just reading about Egypt, why not have the students explore a digital Egyptian museum? Rather than simply read a play by Shakespeare, why not travel, virtually, to the Old Globe or watch an archived production by The Royal Shakespeare Company?

Computers give schools and students a more concrete experience than mere text can allow.

12. **Use more visual search browsers than Google.** The Google gods have us trained to mostly use the main Google page, but the fact is that there are some search browsers out there that are far more visual. Here are some to try:

    Junior Google

    Kiddle.co

    Instagrok

13. **Develop infographics.** Infographics are visual displays of data. You've seen them before in every newspaper and magazine these days. They are one-pagers that combine symbols and images with short chunks of text, data, statistics, and charts. A lot of information can be displayed efficiently and in an engaging way. Students should not only learn how to read infographics, but they should learn to create them too. Use www.Piktochart.com to easily guide students to create these artifacts.

Figure 2.2 is an infographic used to reflect the accomplishments of my middle school for their second annual Invention Convention.

There aren't many givens in this world, but of those that exist, the power of using visuals in a classroom is one of them. However, it's also about input *and* output. Students shouldn't just be asked to watch and view; they also need to be asked to draw and create themselves. Deliver information with visuals to back it up; encourage students to submit their work with visuals to highlight concepts in a different way. The students talk about using visuals as a means toward engagement; but we also know that we should use visuals to help students embed knowledge.

The following Engaging Teacher Spotlight lesson by high school writing teacher Trevor Hershberger incorporates art into a writing assignment. This fellow of the National Writing Project uses paintings as a way to inspire writing about more abstract concepts, thus making the lesson more concrete.

FIGURE 2.2

INVENTION CONVENTION INFOGRAPHIC BY KELLI O

VISUAL LITERACY: PAINTING ANALYSIS AND COMPARISON LESSON

Trevor Hershberger

A BRIEF NOTE ON HERSHBERGER'S LESSON

Using art to help teach literacy might seem like a very specific focus, but when we think that we are all, every teacher in every subject area, responsible for teaching literacy, we have much to learn from those who are finding engaging ways to do so. In the following lesson, Hershberger tackles visual literacy and uses it to leverage a writing lesson on evidence vs. inference. However, using art and visuals overall can help any teacher create a more engaging literacy lesson.

Visual literacy is a different way to teach students how to "read" the world around them using nonwritten forms as actual texts. As you read Hershberger's model English lesson, one that blends works of art into the teaching of writing, think about how visuals can be used in your classroom, and how works of art can be used to support your own standards as well. Think about the following:

How can you use photography to more deeply understand a concept?

How can use you use paintings to highlight a concept?

How does technology make access to art and visuals overall more efficient?

OVERVIEW

Visual literacy, as this type of education is known, is grounded in the understanding that media such as photography, video, painting, sculpture, and other visual forms communicate messages just like written texts. In fact, just like written texts, these visual texts have a point of view, bias, logic, emotion, authorship, and theme.

One strategy that I've implemented with great success in the last year is the integration of visual texts into my text sets. This 2-day lesson begins with an introduction to analyzing visual art and ends with a comparative paragraph about two thematically linked paintings. This lesson might easily adapt to any other grade level by changing the visual texts, requirements, and scaffolds.

STEP-BY-STEP LESSON

I began the lesson by telling students that they would be analyzing a painting. This would be a bit different than reading a written text, I warned them, but they could still "read" the painting by focusing on its details. The painting I chose for this first exercise was Frank Bramley's 1888 oil on canvas *Hopeless Dawn,* because of its dramatic characters and use of light and shadow (Figure 2.4).

As an introduction, I told my students they would have 10 minutes to gaze at the painting, recording every concrete detail they could see. I did not tell my students anything about the painting, including its title or when it was painted.

Then, I displayed the art on the Interactive Whiteboard and distributed a copy to each student via Google Classroom so they could adjust lighting, zoom in, etc.

FIGURE 2.3

HOPELESS DAWN (1888) BY FRANK BRAMLEY

PD-UK Gov

After an astonishingly quiet 10 minutes, during which I periodically encouraged students to "just keep looking" and "write down *literally every detail*" they noticed, I asked them to compare lists. I encouraged students to cross out anything they had written that was an interpretation rather than an observable detail.

After a few minutes of this, I invited students to share some of their observations. Sometimes, a student would suggest an inference rather than a detail. These instances were welcome teachable moments that allowed students to better understand the difference between inference and evidence.

Next, we repeated this exercise with a new painting that I shared via Classroom. Again, I did not share with students the name of this painting—*Stormy Sky Over the Bay*, a 2013 watercolor on paper by Jean Lurssen (Figure 2.5)—but simply gave them 10 minutes again to record every detail they could discern in this very different painting.

On the next day, we all accessed our digital copies of each painting along with the paintings' titles, years, media, and artists. After a brief review of the previous day's discussions, I presented students with the following prompt:

FIGURE 2.4

STORMY SKY OVER THE BAY (2013) BY JEAN LURSSEN

*While oceans feature in both **Hopeless Dawn** and **Stormy Sky Over the Bay**, Bramley's ocean is a background character in **Hopeless Dawn**, while Lurssen's is front and center in her painting. Still, both paintings may be interpreted as characterizing the ocean similarly.*

What aspect of the ocean do both painters seem to agree upon? How does each painter communicate this message about the ocean? Consider details such as color, light and shadow, the position, size, and number of people and objects, etc.

*Write a well-developed **paragraph** that compares the techniques each painter uses to portray the ocean in a particular light. Be sure to cite specific details from each painting as evidence to support your claim. Your paragraph should have a topic sentence with your main claim, several concrete details from each painting, appropriate transitions, and a concluding sentence.*

Next, I handed students the graphic organizer shown in Figure 2.5 that helped them to identify "implied or overt qualities" the two paintings' oceans have in common. Figure 2.5 is available for download on the companion website. At the end of the period, I received full paragraphs from every student—a feat not always accomplished by this group of students in prior writing tasks.

REFLECTION

A large majority of my students quickly picked up on the idea that paintings are not just pretty things to look at passively, but texts that they can read actively and from which they can discern a message or meaning. By offering students a different kind of text to analyze—one that didn't have the linguistic obstacles of a written text—I saw *every* student engaged in my lesson, writing observations, talking productively with partners, and literally pointing out the details from each painting that they could later use as evidence in their paragraphs. My English learners were just as engaged as my students who have grown up in English-only homes, and they met the learning goals about as well, too.

The following student response typifies the kind of responses I got from my solid-B students like Sean. Minor grammatical faults aside, this response made me so excited. By bringing more visual texts into my class in the future, I hope not only to support

FIGURE 2.5

IMPLIED VERSUS OVERT QUALITIES GRAPHIC ORGANIZER

Pre-Writing Planning Chart
Thesis: *What implied or overt quality do the two painters' oceans have in common?*

Supporting Evidence (Concrete Details)	
Hopeless Dawn (Bramley)	*Stormy Sky Over the Bay* (Lurssen)

my students in becoming more visually literate, but also to continue to build the analytical skills they need to transfer to their readings of written texts.

STUDENT WORK

The two painters seem to agree that the ocean is gloomy and somewhat ominous. One example of this in Bramley's painting is that he put the two sad women next to the ocean, which looks grey and depressing. Which suggests that the ocean evokes sadness or despair. First, in Lurssen's painting, he has the boat in the middle of the almost stormy looking ocean. This implies that something bad will happen to the small sailboat. Another example in Bramley's is that even though most of the painting's light, gloomy and unsatisfying, comes from the window, it is still dark outside. Making the people sad and the general emotion of the painting sad. Second, in Lurssen's, the sky and the ocean are so seemingly sad and stormy that the sun can't even break through the clouds. Lurssen may be trying to convey hopelessness through this detail. A final example in Bramley's is that the waves are crashing and it shows that there may be a storm coming. Finally, it looks as though the clouds are rolling in, and the waves, peaks white, are crashing heavier. This shows that there is a storm coming. Both paintings thus feel as though the ocean is somber and sad.

DISCUSSION QUESTIONS

1. How do you use technology to guide students to both consume information and create artifacts of their knowledge?

2. How might you incorporate paintings, photographs, or other forms of art into your classroom content as our Spotlight teacher did? How might you use portraits in math class or landscapes in history class?

3. What determines a quality YouTube, Brainpop, or Khan Academy video in your opinion? What is the criteria that you personally have developed in assessing what supplemental visual can help support your students' learning?

4. Think of your favorite, albeit more traditionally crafted, lesson. How might you modify this beloved lesson to include technology and/or visuals?

Photo courtesy of Davis Lester

CHAPTER THREE

CONNECT WHAT WE LEARN TO THE WORLD

"Apply what I learn to real life . . ."

OVERVIEW

We aren't in the business of preparing our students to take tests for the rest of their lives. We aren't in the business of helping our students learn to navigate school as the end-all, be-all model of life's journey. Nope. As Jeff Wilhelm (2016) reminds us in a Writing Project keynote, "We're in this to develop tools to use in the real world."

Imagine a classroom where students are cast as inventors trying to solve the irksome problems of everyday life. Through research, drafting, prototyping, and presentation, one student pitches a product that helps with the tangled wires underneath a desk. Another finds a way to collect the condensation from a shower curtain. And yet another student develops a shoe that can dispel a temporary sole after stepping in dog poo. They develop commercials to promote their inventions, and these are posted on the school website for all to see.

> "Imagine a classroom that takes what students learn about their country and challenges small groups to create their own."

Imagine a classroom that takes what students learn about their country and challenges small groups to create their own. The students decide on the boundaries of their new nation, its laws, and its goals for its people. These new colonists role-play as geologists, policy makers, economists, and contractors to develop the infrastructure and systems that help build a successful nation. They develop a constitution and trade agreements between the countries in the classroom.

> "I think the main problem with learning is that teachers don't connect it to real life. . . . Most of the things we learn aren't "useful" in real life. Math, maybe . . . English maybe . . . But the majority of them aren't directly related to real life. . . . Also some teachers stick to the book, which can be boring."
>
> —Laron N., Middle Schooler

Imagine a classroom that is given the task to save a species, a mythical creature that proves vital to its environment. The students Skype with zoologists. They write executive summaries to legislators that include infographics to help them visualize researched data focusing on the creature's habitat and the interdependency of multiple species within that environment. Students create a social media campaign to protect the species.

This is a window into meaningful learning, lessons that connect to the life outside of school. This is a window into project-based learning.

When you are first developing a PBL unit, you must begin the journey by establishing an authentic goal. By the end of the unit, you want students to have solved something. Along the way, they will have written, collaborated, created, pitched, discussed, and presented.

"Project-based learning (PBL) differs from a project by addressing another concept that many students mentioned, that of ensuring that learning is more meaningful and applicable to real-life scenarios."

ENGAGE WITH THE CONTENT

This video synthesizes themes in our teacher and student interviews that focused on leveraging role play to help students get into their units of study. Using role-playing helps break down the walls between school life and the life outside our walls. As you watch the video, think about the following:

- How does becoming a character aid in learning?
- What units of study could you begin by establishing a character that students can embody?
- At what age does role-playing stop being engaging? (*Note:* That's a trick question; you're never too old to pretend!)

Video 3.1 Engage Through Role-Playing

One-shot projects tend to reinforce other engaging strategies mentioned in this book, namely more visual learning and more hands-on learning. However, PBL differs from a project by addressing another concept that many students mentioned, that of ensuring that learning is more meaningful and applicable to real-life scenarios.

PBL focuses on students having an impact on the world around them, and as such, they know that much of what they learn

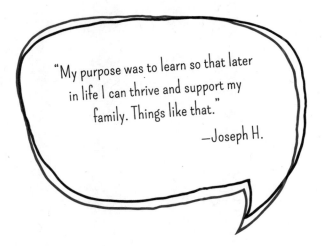

"My purpose was to learn so that later in life I can thrive and support my family. Things like that."

—Joseph H.

> "I like to physically apply what I learn in real life. One of my favorite math teachers would take us to go do measurements of actual structures to figure out area, finding missing lengths, and apply theorems."
>
> —Quoc B., Tenth Grade

> "Another thing I really like is when they connect classes that most students think, 'Oh, well, I'm definitely not going to use this later in life, I'll just forget all about it as soon as I'm out of school,' to real-life situations."
>
> —Coleen C.

can be applied to the world outside the walls of school. For these reasons, PBL is known to be one of the most engaging methods of student learning because it is meaningful to the students themselves.

This is vital because PBL requires a lot of critical thinking from the student, and this can cause a student's brain to sweat in effort. However, only if it's meaningful will students embrace the effort it takes to pursue the unit's goals.

I have long been a supporter of PBL. To many, that's project-based learning. To others, it's problem-based learning. Of course, let's not forget passion-based learning, inquiry-based learning, service-based learning, and so on. Regardless of the term, they all include the following devices:

Real-world application

Role play

Driven by inquiry (either posed by teacher or student created)

Authentic audience

Group work, individual assessment

Outside expertise brought into classroom

Student voice

Student choice, highly differentiated

Assessing the journey, not just the final outcome

"Published" product

Oral, visual, text-based presentation

Integrating tech

21st Century Skills: creativity, collaboration, communication, critical thinking

I begin this chapter talking about my passion for PBL because one of the reasons why it is so effective in engaging students is because it is also effective in engaging teachers. Engagement, you see, is contagious. Author Hal White (n.d.) notes, "Much of the enthusiasm for the problem-based approach to learning comes from instructors who feel revitalized by the creative energy it releases."

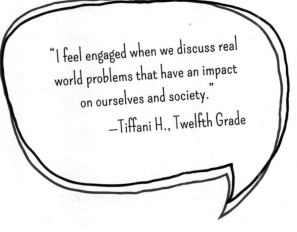

"I feel engaged when we discuss real world problems that have an impact on ourselves and society."

—Tiffani H., Twelfth Grade

To teacher trainer Andrew Miller, PBL teachers are "rockstars who harness and hone" six skills simultaneously: They typically tend to be collaborative, give power to students, are "learning environment designers," are student centered, honor 21st Century Skills, and plan (Miller, 2012).

As a result of teachers adopting such mindsets, the students also learn more deeply. In a 2016 study by MDRC/Lucas Education Research, the authors of *Project-Based Learning: A Literature Review* found "that the design principles most commonly used in PBL align well with the goals of preparing students for deeper learning, higher-level thinking skills, and intra/interpersonal skills" (Vega, 2012).

These skills allow teachers to take a step back and enjoy the development of their students. They can observe a journey of learning that traditional teaching can disallow.

As a PBL teacher, I know that I wake up every day excited to see what my students will come up with. I'm never bored. And as such, my excitement is passed on to my students.

PBL ISN'T JUST ABOUT ENGAGEMENT; IT'S ALSO ABOUT ACHIEVEMENT

"I feel like we should learn about things that actually would support us in the outside world."

—Liam M., Seventh Grade

When we talk about PBL, we focus our curriculum on finding real-world ways for students to learn problem-solving and communication skills. When doing this, authenticity is key. According to the National Education Association, as far back as the early 1900s, John Dewey supported the "learning by doing" approach to education, which is the essential element of PBL. . . . Today, PBL is viewed as a model for classroom activity that shifts away from teacher-centered instruction and emphasizes student-centered projects. . . . This model helps make learning relevant to students by establishing connections to life outside the classroom and by addressing real world issues. (National Education Association, n.d.)

> "When I'm learning about something that is a world issue. When I'm learning about something that affects me directly or something related to what I want to do later in life."
>
> —Matthew A., Twelfth Grade

A 2001 Stanford newsletter reported that Dr. Renate Fruchter (n.d.), the founding director of its PBL lab, shared that past students reach out to her once they have been employed. "I can tell you tons of stories," she says, which I have been kind of informally collecting over the years. Many times [students] . . . treat school . . . like . . . [it] is just a simulation. Then they go out and they are in situations which are almost identical to the ones they have experienced in the lab. The learning experience was so valuable because it prepared them to handle, anticipate . . . and prevent some of the miscommunications and difficult situations emerging on every project.

PBL promotes that kind of real-world simulation even in the K–12 classroom.

And the correlation with PBL and student achievement isn't merely celebrated in anecdotes. Studies have shown that these kinds of units improve long-term information retention, skill development, and student satisfaction (Strobel, & van Barneveld, 2009).

In fact, in 2002, a study was conducted between two British secondary schools. The study found that "students in the project-based-learning school significantly outperformed the traditional-school students in mathematics skills as well as conceptual and applied knowledge. In fact, in the project-based-learning school, three times as many students passed the national exam" (Boaler, 2002).

Another study focused on a particular project-based economics unit that was taught to approximately 7,000 twelfth graders in 66 high schools. The students who participated "outscored their peers in the control group who received the more typical textbook—and lecture-driven approach. . . . Students also scored higher on measures of problem-solving skills and their application to real-world economic challenges" (U.S. Department of Education, 2011).

But I'm not going to lie; PBL can feel overwhelming to start. For that reason, I want to deconstruct it a bit so that it can be digested into more bite-sized pieces to chew on and enjoy.

ENGAGE WITH THE CONTENT

The video to the right highlights how PBL embraces real-world learning. While there are many elements to PBL that you can bring in that help make your lessons more authentic, PBL blends them into a cohesive unit chock-full of meaning. As you watch the interviews and classroom interaction, think about the following:

- How can PBL be used for every subject area?

- What would you need to feel supported in order to tackle developing your own PBL unit?

- What are the elements of school that traditionally do not reflect life outside of school? Why do you think these elements remain in use?

Video 3.2 Connect Learning to the Real World

BREAKING DOWN THE PARTS OF PBL

Here's a good place to start: Plan to have students imagine themselves as different characters, professions, facilitators, or experts.

Now think about what you want them to accomplish at the end of the unit.

The lessons, activities, and mini-projects or assessments fill in the spaces between the launch and the culmination.

"I think of PBL as a story, a narrative of curriculum."

Make sure to plan a reflection at the end of the unit so that students can look back over their journey.

That's it. Simple, right? OK, I'm exaggerating. There's more to PBL than that, but that's the basic structure.

In terms of pacing, teachers have tackled PBL in many different ways. Some designate a day per week as their PBL period. Others select a time of year when testing is done and they have more freedom in their curriculum choices. However, real PBL can be integrated during the class any time of year, on any day, because it helps deliver the content that needs to be taught.

For instance, while my eighth-grade department all teaches narrative during the first quarter of school, I have my students begin to develop science-based origin stories for their original superhero unit. The standards are hit, but the container that delivers those standards keeps to our "What makes a hero?" superhero PBL unit.

No matter the pacing, the purpose remains the same: Bring more meaningful learning into the classroom.

Throughout the unit, students also begin to develop more independence, a skill that is required outside of school as well. Students participating in a PBL unit will adopt the learning process themselves without depending on the teacher to simply bring them information on a plate. You see, PBL transfers the teaching from the teacher to the student. Meanwhile, the teacher assesses the journey of learning rather than simply the end result. This means that the formal "teaching" is replaced by surreptitiously guiding students toward what they need to learn to accomplish a goal. This could look like so many things:

- Asking probing questions rather than answering them
- Having students bring in examples of a particular standard rather than providing them yourself
- Developing scaffolds for different levels of learners that are available to all who need them, and are accessed independently rather than prescribed by the teacher

By sitting shotgun in the passenger seat of what's being "taught," teachers therefore encourage students to develop their own skills as content-area experts.

I think of PBL as a story, a narrative of curriculum. If we adopt the theory that a PBL unit paces itself like a story of learning, the basic steps might look like this:

Exposition—State a content-based question. The teacher provides an open-ended question that needs to be solved or the students develop their own question. PBL is about triggering curiosity. And activating a student's curiosity is, I would argue, a far more important and complex goal than the objective of mere information delivery. Some believe this can be easier on teachers because it transfers some responsibilities from teachers to students, but the fact is that it's really easier because students are more engaged to learn. The power of the question should help drive student research, the writing, and the presentation. It should help motivate them to become experts in their little self-described field. And the more often a student gets a taste of what it feels like to be an expert, in however small a concept, the more they will want that feeling later on in life. Hear the new ideas they bring to the table on problems that range from local issues to global ones. Have them develop questions about how things are run, and challenge why our systems can't be different.

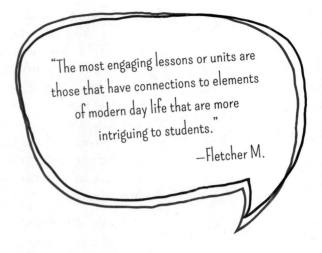

"The most engaging lessons or units are those that have connections to elements of modern day life that are more intriguing to students."

—Fletcher M.

- Students can write pitches (informal assessment opportunity), develop roles, and be put into collaborative groups.

- Students can set their own norms and develop rubrics on which they will be assessed later.

- Students can brainstorm in writing the ways in which they can help their world or their local community. They can check out Newsela, CNN Student News, or their local papers for articles on current events and issues of interest to get in informational reading, as well.

Rising Action—Research the topic using time in class. It's crucial to have some of this be classwork so students have access to the head researcher in the room—the teacher. Remember, the teacher doesn't do the work for them, but is going to guide them and model methods of researching reliably. Have them find the research to back-up their theories. Students learn Internet literacy skills and ways to research reliably. Students learn about citation (which should be included on all assignments). Experts can be brought into the classroom or interviews conducted. Have students develop surveys (informal assessment based on inquiry) to crowdsource advice from others. Have students synthesize their findings in multiple ways chosen by the students themselves. Perhaps they can develop an infographic (informal assessment) using Piktochart to marry data, text, and symbols to prove their stance through a more visual presentation of evidence.

Climax—Students present what they've learned. Students should create and present a culminating artifact. When I have my students present what they've learned, I use a rubric that uses "Able to Teach" as the acme of what to reach for. After all, many people can understand content, but can they communicate it? Have them present and publish their research-based thoughts and solutions. Have them create the items that will make our lives easier, more efficient, and more enjoyable. Have them design, print, make, write about, and speak about their solutions. Students can develop their own assessments such as these:

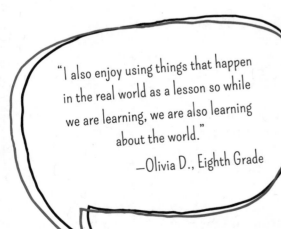

"I also enjoy using things that happen in the real world as a lesson so while we are learning, we are also learning about the world."

—Olivia D., Eighth Grade

- Websites as portfolios of their work to publicize their solutions

- Slideshows

- TEDTalk or Ignite speeches

- Posters to promote their call to action,

- Letter-writing campaigns

- "Road tours" to local schools and organizations to share their findings

- Screencasts for the school website

Falling Action—Ask students to reflect on what worked about the process and what didn't. Generally specific to inquiry-based learning, there is an element of post-unit reflection of what was learned and how one grew from the learning experience. Reflection is key. And it isn't just about asking them to think back on their opinion of the topic. It's about reflecting on the process itself. That's where you can work in metacognition. Thinking about thinking. Thinking about *how* they learned not just *what* they learned.

- Students can create Google Forms for crowdsourced feedback on their presentations or read reviews from those in their audience.
- Students can assess data based on their outreach.

Resolution—Rubrics are filled out by multiple stakeholders. Many times, in particular to service-based learning, an element of the final assessment involves all of the stakeholders involved. In other words, while the teacher might be involved, both the student and the outside community member with whom the student worked for/with, all are given an opportunity to assess the effectiveness of the students' efforts.

Notice that the unit is an entire journey. It is not a one-shot project. There are projects peppered throughout, but they become variables to the entire equation of learning.

TeachThought.org says the following in support of this:

> In PBL, the projects only serve as an infrastructure to allow users to play, experiment, use simulations, address authentic issues, and work with relevant peers and community members in pursuit of knowledge. . . . By design, PBL is learner-centered. Students don't simply choose between two highly academic projects to complete by a given date, but instead use the teacher's experience to design and iterate products and projects–products and projects that often address issues or challenges that are important to them. ("The Difference Between Projects and Project-Based Learning," 2012)

And when learning is important to them, the effort it takes to produce outcomes is more meaningful for the student and more authentic.

FINDING AN AUTHENTIC GOAL FOR YOUR PBL UNIT

The key to a great PBL unit is in developing the initial question or goal. That goal becomes the launching pad to the learning. Finding an authentic goal helps to merge student experiences with real-world applications. It embraces both standards-based instruction with student-centered and independent learning. It doesn't forsake the content, but rather, provides a more engaging and meaningful vehicle from which to learn it.

Jim Bentley (2016), a middle school teacher and National Faculty Member for the Buck Institute of Education, an organization devoted to educating teachers and providing resources developed around PBL, says,

> What makes a PBL unit of study truly meaningful in my opinion is whether or not the project is authentic. When kids perceive the work they're doing as real, as making a difference, as something that is adding value to the world, they're hooked.

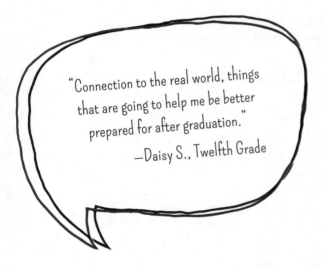

"Connection to the real world, things that are going to help me be better prepared for after graduation."

—Daisy S., Twelfth Grade

Many students have learned how school works: teachers talk, students listen, teachers assign, students complete, teachers assess, students get results. In a PBL classroom, that traditional cycle that's been around since the advent of schools is turned upside down. When students see a teacher struggling and working alongside them as a co-learner, the fundamental nature of the teacher-student relationship is transformed. I refer to my students as "co-workers," and I'm adopting the term of lead-learner for myself rather than "teacher." I find on a daily basis students are the ones teaching me new things.

There is great power in discovering the needs of your own community, and teachers have a role to play in helping students ask the questions to discover what those needs are. This process of inquiry is both the initial, and most essential part, of any PBL unit.

For instance, earlier this year, I helped a colleague learn about PBL. We decided (based on her own interest in marathons) to have her English language arts class host a 5K Fun Run fundraiser for a local charity. Her kids weren't the ones running, however. Instead, they were meeting with the timing company, developing the registration website, pitching sponsors, working on mapping the course, and meeting with the city to seek approvals on the process.

They settled on a local charity by researching from a list of local organizations. In small groups, they started researching using a hyperdoc the teacher had curated. They watched videos, examined documents, and each group created a Google slideshow about their charity to pitch to their class.

Helping the community plays a key part in making any unit more authentic. What's more authentic then seeing if one's studies actually successfully helped those you set out to aide?

With that in mind, I reached out to Rich Lehrer, who was the first e-NABLE Educators Exchange Coordinator—as well as the Innovation Coordinator at the Brookwood School in Massachusetts. The e-NABLE community has been designing and 3D-printing prosthetics for children and has recently created curriculum for PBL units that have been embraced by schools, clubs, hobbyists, and other organizations. He offered some advice on how teachers can find authentic objectives in their own backyard.

1. **Search Online.** Google *PBL + Authentic Projects*. Also try searching the Buck Institute for Education website for project ideas using the key word *authentic*. There's a treasure trove of lists out there.

2. **Have an Authentic Project Mindset.** Seek outlets for authentic work in your life and in the lives your students. Sometimes a goal can be found in the stories and experiences of those found in your own classroom.

3. **Make connections.** "Connect with individuals and organizations in your community and around the world who are doing meaningful work and having tangible effects," recommends Lehrer. Involve your students in the

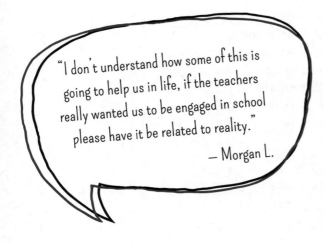

"I don't understand how some of this is going to help us in life, if the teachers really wanted us to be engaged in school please have it be related to reality."

— Morgan L.

work that is already going on in the world. How can we be of service? Lehrer stresses, "As the world becomes more connected, there are amazing chances for kids to do meaningful things."

Help your students develop a sense of their own power. Allow them in on the decision-making process in terms of selecting an authentic goal for your class's PBL unit, and you will have increased their ownership of the unit from the get-go.

"Kids have never been as empowered to change their local community than ever before," Rich Lehrer continues.

> Schools are now recognizing that this is vital for student development, that there is much educational value in this, and that kids now have access to the tools to make long-lasting advocacy happen.

> We need our students to think of themselves as change agents in this world. They have access to the devices to help that happen, but now they need access to teachers willing to take them on that journey. (as quoted to Wolpert-Gawron, 2016)

"We need our students to think of themselves as change agents in this world."

For not only does PBL encourage rigorous content-area learning, it also enfolds the learners in lessons on empathy and advocacy. Tim Holt (2013), blogger for the Powerful Learning Practice, says,

> Let's face it. For generations, we have almost completely bypassed the development of true problem solving skills in our curricula. Now it's something that the "real world" is clamoring for us to incorporate into our lessons. (How many times have we heard the phrase "We need problem solvers!") And it's something that's likely going to be incorporated in the testing, not very far down the road. . . . We have also left out ethical considerations in curricula. It's not about telling kids *what* to think. It's about getting them TO think when it comes to issues of right and wrong. This, I think, is a goal that Problem Based Learning can readily help us reach.

PBL is a strategy of learning that proves to be a huge proponent of engagement. It's about leveraging the need to do something good in the world as a means to help kids hit their learning objectives. It's about teaching empathy as well as literacy. It's about teaching compassion as well as composition. It's about teaching advocacy as well as algebra.

WHAT MEANINGFUL LEARNING LOOKS LIKE IN THE CLASSROOM

I know I've focused a great deal on PBL in this chapter, but that's because it packages many meaningful elements all within a single unit of study. However, if we tease apart those elements, we can see just how a classroom can engage through more real-life applicable learning. Here are just some of the ways you can help make learning more meaningful. I'm calling them different "points of engagement."

> "I feel like we should learn things that go with what career we want, not things that might not even help us in our adult life. . . . Teach us what to do when we're adults, like how to pay taxes, buy a house, buy a car, etc. that can actually help us when we're older."
>
> —Sierra F.

1. **Bring in an outside expert into your classroom.**
   Regardless of what your content area may be, one of the best ways to make learning more authentic is to bring in experts from the professional world into your classroom. They can come in face-to-face or Skype in. Reach out to parents, alumni, your friends and family, or even your dentist. As the myth says, we're all six-degrees away from each other, so tap into your network to find people to contribute their knowledge and experience. Reach out to museums and local laboratories; many of these kinds of organizations have educational outreach branches but don't know which classrooms are looking for their input. Make your needs known within your community and bring meaning to your students' learning.

2. **Involve an authentic audience to help assess student achievement.** Many times, it's only the teacher who sees the end result of a student's work. But far more engaging is when there is another audience that has some

kind of relationship with the material. Perhaps it's other members of the educational community who come in to view or evaluate the student artifacts: the principal or the Board of Education. Perhaps it's the recipient of a project, the senior citizens from the nearby home who students worked with, or business leaders and politicians from the local community who want to see their newest constituents' ideas. Fold in the outside world into every step of the learning process, even the final one.

ENGAGE WITH THE CONTENT

The video to the right talks about the importance of using an authentic audience to aid in student learning. After all, the teacher's voice should not be the end-all, be-all authority; students should be learning from many, not just from one. As you listen to the teacher and hear what various students have to say, think about the following:

Video 3.3 Tap Into Authentic Audiences

- Who do you know that you can bring in to help advise students?
- Does bringing in an authentic audience downgrade the teacher's voice any or merely recast it in a different role?
- Are people from outside the classroom obligated to solely give advice on classroom standards, or do they bring in different standards entirely?
- How can you use rubrics to help outside audiences calibrate to your own standards?

3. **Base learning on questions related to life outside of school.** Depending on your comfort and the focus of the unit, expert opinion varies on whether student-developed or teacher-developed questions are more meaningful as a means to instigate initial investigations in a PBL unit. Regardless, however, those questions need to be based in actual issues that exist outside of school. Yes, student-developed questions are perhaps more meaningful to the student, but the questions also need to be meaningful to the material, and sometimes that takes teacher influence. What's vital, however, is that the driving questions come from life: what's going on in current events, what's happened in the past, and what connects to the students themselves.

4. **Desegregate the content areas.**
   It's true. Blending subject areas is far more authentic and connected to the real world than our current silos of learning. Let's face it; scientists still have to pitch their discoveries in writing and speaking. Writers still communicate beyond literature. It's also just as important to blend genres of writing. In the real world, a persuasive speech includes anecdote as much as it might include data. An email might analyze and breakdown a prediction and try to persuade toward a particular response. Nothing in real life is separated into categories; instead, they are blended and mixed. The only way students can apply and transfer what they learn is if they learn they also can't escape tapping into any lesson at any time.

"For me, what engages me as a student in the classroom correlates to learning about real world and issues that are present and need to be addressed."

—Heather C., Middle Schooler

ENGAGING TEACHER SPOTLIGHT

Diane Tom is a middle school science teacher from Los Angeles, California. She has also spent six summers volunteering for the National Park Service (NPS) as a teacher ranger and volunteer in parks. This following PBL unit was a magnificent marriage of her interest with her content area.

FIND YOUR PARK

OVERVIEW

Little did I know what would result when I decided to share my passion for America's national parks with my seventh-grade students. Informal classroom surveys confirmed what Richard Louv wrote about in his book *Last Child in the Woods*—a majority of my students are suffering from nature-deficit disorder. Most have had no personal experience with our beloved national parks. A well-known local event is the Tournament of Roses Parade every

January 1, and the 2016 parade theme was chosen to honor the 100th anniversary of the NPS. With the entire nation celebrating the NPS centennial, the perfect opportunity existed to connect the real world to my classroom—my students would study ecology science standards through the creation of national park parade float models.

1. Students were put into heterogeneous collaborative groups that were each assigned a park.

2. Groups researched the specific challenges faced by each park and developed a call-to-action for the public to solve those problems.

3. In order to complete their projects, the students needed a rich background in national parks and the Rose Parade. They used NPS websites to discover why people consider the national parks to be "America's best idea," and they gained a more personal perspective with my park ranger friend on Skype.

4. Firsthand knowledge was also absolutely essential, so I planned a field trip to the nearest NPS site as a shared experience. Our field trip to the Santa Monica National Recreation Area (SAMO) consisted of four different activities: (a) removing invasive crayfish from the waterways with a non-profit environmental organization, (b) hiking different trails to experience the outdoors, (c) studying the park's natural history at the Visitor's Center, and (d) connecting with the national park rangers and staff. At the end of the very long day, the students presented the park staff with our class donation money. The rangers swore everyone in as Junior Rangers and awarded SAMO collectible badges, with the expectation that the students would be future caretakers of our national parks.

5. After the field trip, each student selected a memorable nature observation to research and present to the class in the form of a haiku poem.

6. Groups emailed their parks for expert ranger advice.

7. Each student created an informational poster about a specific park topic and all the students participated in a gallery walk.

8. To become knowledgeable about the Rose Parade, the students researched online, viewed actual floats at different stages of construction, and interviewed the tournament president during his classroom visit.

9. The groups planned their miniature parade floats to represent their park habitats and an environmental challenge threatening the park.

10. In the end, the school tweeted out pictures of the floats including call-to-actions developed by the students for each park represented.

During the course of this unit, my purpose was to not only inspire them to create personal connections with the national parks, but to also discover real-world examples of the ecological principles we were studying in our science curriculum.

REFLECTION

My "behind-the-scenes" knowledge of the NPS and my network of friends enabled me to creatively tap into park and tournament resources to create both a unique curriculum unit and a memorable life experience for my students. Former students come up to me to ask if I am still taking field trips into the national parks. Because of the frontloading and student involvement prior to the field trip, the students felt prepared, confident, and eager to be outdoors. Experiencing a park together with their peers established a common ground that encouraged student buy-in throughout the rest of the national parks unit. Even more important was establishing a personal connection with nature and planting the seeds for the next generation of park visitors and stewards.

The students were tremendously engaged during all aspects of the unit, and they frequently surprised me by going beyond my expectations in the work they produced. Students who struggled with more traditional textbook-based lessons blossomed into active collaborators due to the variety of assignments and their interest in the parks. I had an overflowing crowd of students and parents attend our float Open House event and I could feel their excitement as we awaited the judges' announcements about which floats won awards. By a happy coincidence, the NPS sponsored a Virtual Rose Parade competition through Twitter prior to the actual Rose Parade. We entered our float projects into the contest and watched as we not only won the Junior Ranger Award, but also national recognition and praise from some of the actual parks we portrayed.

I know that many of my students share my passion for the national parks. They (and sometimes even their parents) tell me about their summer park visits and return with gifts of park memorabilia. Although there are many heartwarming entries written by students in my yearbook, one of my favorites is "I think my favorite part of the ENTIRE school year (including every class) was going on the park field trip."

DISCUSSION QUESTIONS

1. Ask yourself honestly, how comfortable are you with permitting students to develop driving questions that will guide the learning, or are you more comfortable developing a choice of questions instead?

2. How might you assess how meaningful a lesson or unit might be? How many points of engagement can you trigger within a particular lesson or unit?

3. If PBL is like telling a story via curriculum, what characters or roles might students be able to adopt that relate to your content area?

4. Think of your favorite, albeit more traditionally crafted, lesson. How might you modify this beloved lesson to bring in an expert from outside of school or a more authentic audience to help assess student learning?

Photo courtesy of Davis Lester

CHAPTER FOUR

LET US MOVE AROUND

"It helps when teachers let us move around."

OVERVIEW

....

Kinesthetic learning is about moving one's body in order to help better embed understanding. It can leverage both complex and simple movement so that a concept does not get quickly relegated to short-term memory.

Many teachers have heard about kinesthetic learning through the theories of Howard Gardner's multiple intelligences. And indeed, there are students out there who show an instinct and tendency toward needing movement in order to learn or show their learning. For instance, Milo P., a middle schooler from the northwest stated in the Student Engagement Survey that without a doubt, "P.E engages me the most because there is friendly competition and you are always moving, being active etc. It's never boring and gives you great exercise." This is a student who clearly loves the class that has the most movement.

I bring up Milo because there are Milos in every classroom, those kids who are looking out the window and can't wait for the bell so that they can go to PE or recess or their after school sport. What we want to learn about in this chapter, however, is how we can take advantage of a student's desire to move as a means to help teach our content area. What we're talking about here goes beyond what a particular student's tendency might be, and asks teachers to begin to capitalize on movement as a means to engage all learners.

In *The Importance of Learning Styles: Understanding the Implications for Learning, Course Design, and Education,* Ronald and Serbenia Simms claim that kinesthetic learners, "require whole body movement . . . and learn most easily when they are totally involved. Acting, puppetry, and drama, are excellent examples of kinesthetic learning; others include building, designing, visiting, interviewing, and playing" (Sims & Sims, 1995).

"What engages me as a student is when we have interactive activities because associating a lesson with activity helps it stick in my mind. Ms Mills had an activity on World War One where we would would see the effects of the war in paper balls where we would collect them to see how we fared in the war."

—Jacob B., Tenth Grade

It's important to note here that some research blends kinesthetic learning with the additional nomenclature of "hands on" learning, but for the purposes of this book, we're teasing it apart here because of the students' responses. The students seem to recognize, as many researchers do, that movement of body is different from simply encouraging a more tactile approach.

Movement in the classroom wakes them up.

Movement in the classroom helps them to release stress, which "lowers the drawbridge" to allow learning in.

Movement in the classroom helps concepts to "stick" better by attaching whole body action to a particular topic.

Putting the academic research aside, our real experts, the students, know this to be true as well.

Let's face it, we all get antsy sometimes, and even as an adult, I can't even imagine sitting still for 45 minutes to 90 minutes, class after class, with only the passing period in between classes to get out my own bodily boredom.

But their opinion of what helps them learn is also backed up by research. We know, for instance, that exercise increases blood flow to the brain. So there are many benefits to kinesthetic learning as it supports the need for oxygenation to the brain in order to maximize cognitive functioning. In other words, if you want to achieve, we have to let them get up and out of their seats.

Justin Rhodes, an associate professor of psychology at the University of Illinois at Urbana-Champaign, explains in a response to a 2013 claim in *Scientific American* that when we move, "blood pressure and blood flow increase everywhere in the body, including the brain. More blood means more energy and oxygen, which makes our brain perform better" (Rhodes, 2017).

Eric Jensen, in his *The Brain in Mind* gets more technical about why this increase in oxygen has a direct line to learning. "We know exercise fuels the brain with

"I feel like it helps when the teachers let you move around in one part of class. Even if it is just for a few minutes it gives us something to look forward to and a chance to get our wiggles out."

—Eliza J., Sixth Grade

"I am not a type of kid to learn something from just sitting down and trying to learn something out of a book. I need to actually do it."

—Curt W., Junior High Schooler

"One of my teachers even does physical demonstrations to help learn complicated scientific concepts, like having the students stand and assigning one to be the sun and one to be the earth and such."

—Xochipilli A., Twelfth Grade

oxygen, but it also feeds it neurotropins (high-nutrient chemical 'packages') to increase the number of connections between neurons. Most astonishingly, exercise is known to increase the baseline of new neuron growth" (Jensen, 2005).

And there is research to back up kinesthetic strategies as a means to increase student achievement. Anne Green Gilbert, author of *Teaching the Three Rs Through Movement and Creative Dance Across All Ages*, conducted a study in the 1970s in the Seattle Public Schools to assess movement on test scores. She writes the following:

> During the 1977 school year, 250 students from four elementary schools studied language arts concepts through movement and dance activities for twenty weeks. The third grade students involved in the study increased their MAT scores by 13 percent from fall to spring, while the district wide average showed a decrease of 2 percent! The primary grade project students also showed a great improvement in test scores. Most significant was the direct relationship the research showed between the amount of movement the classroom teacher used and the percentage increase of students' test scores. (Green Gilbert, 1997)

"Most significant was the direct relationship the research showed between the amount of movement the classroom teacher used and the percentage increase of students' test scores."

—Anne Green Gilbert, author

In fact, the CDC also produced a study that collected research from many different sources on the effectiveness of physical activity and learning as a means to help advise schools. In their report, "The Association Between School-Based Physical Activity, Including Physical Education, and Academic Performance," they write that

> participating in physical activity was positively related to outcomes including academic achievement, academic behaviors, and indicators of cognitive skills and attitudes, such as concentration, memory, self-esteem, and verbal skills. . . . The majority of these articles (86%) found at least one positive association with academic behavior outcomes. (CDC, 2010)

Unfortunately, even though secondary students have statistically a longer attention span than their elementary counterparts—many educators follow the practice of assuming a student's attention span is the equivalent to the age of the student plus 5 minutes—the fact is that the lack of recess and the push to replace PE with seat time is proving detrimental to what we know to be true: that kids of every age need movement if we are to even help them reach that goal of critical attention.

The good news is that there are strategies in every subject area to help teachers bring movement into the lessons and even into informal assessments. And you don't have to embed choreography from the Joffrey Ballet into your middle school American history class or run a Zumba class with your AP calculus students in order to embrace movement in the classroom.

Got Gum?

"I am engaged when i can move around eating something. Or doing game like things."

—Bryan S.

"Being able to chew gum in class can also help us learn or focus better, I know it helps me."

—Selina N.

WHAT MORE MOVEMENT LOOKS LIKE IN THE CLASSROOM

Kinesthetic learning flies in the face of the passivity that traditional lecture brings to the learning table. It goes without saying that it brings with it a more active room, but that activity can embed information far deeper than mere auditory delivery.

So what are simple things you can do to encourage movement in the classroom? For one thing, you can encourage movement in the very environment of the classroom itself.

There are health benefits to certain positions in which we work. James Levine (2015) with the Mayo Clinic states that

> a sedentary lifestyle appears to be detrimental in the long-term. . . . The solution, they say, isn't to sit for six hours at work and then head to the gym afterward, because evidence suggests that the negative effects of extended sitting can't be countered by brief bouts of strenuous exercise. The answer is incorporating standing, pacing and other forms of activity into your normal day.

"Many educators follow the practice of assuming a student's attention span is the equivalent to the age of the student plus 5 minutes."

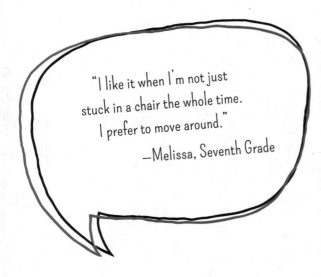

"I like it when I'm not just stuck in a chair the whole time. I prefer to move around."

—Melissa, Seventh Grade

Some studies have shown, for instance, that standing while working might help fight obesity and diabetes. Other studies show that movement while being seated may help with attention, keeping both the brain and the body engaged while in class.

I think about my own seating habits in meetings and workshops. I know, for instance, that I tend to be a "back sitter," one that sits in the back so I can stand and stretch my legs or lean my chair back against the wall to rock a bit (I know, I tell my students not to do it, too). I think about the length of time that I can sit before I need to adjust my position in order to continue my attentiveness. Let me tell, you it isn't that long.

With this in mind, I recently began experimenting with my own classroom environment in a way that allowed for more movement. To do that, I needed an ally, so I approached my principal, and he agreed to switch out some traditional seats with a few video game chairs. I soon noticed that many of my most fidgety students wrote more quantitatively when rocking in the chair than when in their static seat. It became clear to me that when certain learners could repeatedly rock, they would also produce more writing.

Video 4.1 Get Them Moving

ENGAGE WITH THE CONTENT!

This video illustrates many ways to integrate movement into the classroom. Check out the flexible seating in my own ELA classroom, and enter Diane Tom's science classroom where she uses movement as a transition from activity to activity. Also, hear from the students themselves on the topic. No surprise here: Students don't just need to move around; they love it too! As you watch, think about the following:

- How are students showing autonomy through movement?
- When is movement used in the classroom?
- How is movement used to highlight the standards?

We also provided some detached chairs and tables on wheels so that students could move any of them into different positions depending on the activity or the partnerships, as shown in the photos that follow. Sometimes, that just means rolling them around for a different view of the classroom. Other times it means allowing the students to choose the organization that helps the role play of the lesson. The movable desks and chairs can therefore be transformed into a large rectangular table in some mythical CEO's boardroom or the C-shaped amphitheater of the United Nations in only a couple of minutes.

And speaking of different views, I also have a number of standing desks in the classroom because, according to Levine (2015), there are many students who prefer to work standing up rather than sitting down.

Of course, classroom environment is only one way to integrate more movement into your classroom. The real goal, however, is to embed movement into the lessons themselves.

A VIDEO GAME CHAIR IN USE

Photo courtesy of Heather Wolpert-Gawron

Here are some suggestions:

1. **Sixth-Grade Math Place Value Lesson.** Grab a rubber band ball or a stress reducing ball and hand it off to a student who will act as the "decimal." Have a line of students stand in the front of the class, each with a different number assigned to him or her. Have the "decimal" stand between two students and have a student read what the long number the students represent at the front of the classroom. Speak the word *and* when it's the decimal's place in the line. For instance:

   Four thousand, three hundred sixty-one *and* twenty-two hundredths

Now move the student holding the decimal. Have another student read the new number. It might become

   Four hundred, thirty-six *and* one hundred twenty-two thousandths

2. **Four Corners.** This strategy asks students to stand in different corners of the room to show their opinion of a debatable topic. The corners are labeled as *strongly agree, agree, disagree,* and *strongly disagree.* Upon hearing a basic thesis statement, students must then stand in the area that best represents how they feel about the topic. As students learn more about the topic or debate it using evidence, they can move to different corners of the room to show indecision or a changed mind.

3. **Peer Review Stations.** Teachers can set up areas in the classroom that are designated for different purposes. Rather than have worksheets of different activities that get passed out to each student (where it's the papers moving, not the students), the kids themselves can get up and move to the activity area. For instance, when my students revise their essays, there are multiple revision stations. One area will be designated as the place to ask peers for targeted advice. Once a student does that, they can stand and go to another area where you can record your essay on a computer and use headphones to listen to it back to catch errors independently. Another station asks students to exchange papers to color

"I like to do active things, that's how I learn better."

—Jose, Eleventh Grade

code each other's work and write comments in the margins. Sure, this can all be done from a student's seat using Google Drive, but the movement keeps them more alert.

4. **Get up and switch seats.** Once a week, have students get up and rotate their seats, one to the right, or something like that. You can also have a table group switch tables with another group. A change of view does them good!

5. **Use sign language.** Have students learn to speak using their hands. These can be recognized signs used in American Sign Language, like "May I go to the restroom?" or it can be signs you've, as a class, made up to accomplish certain goals of communication. For instance, rather than simply having them raise their hands, they can put one hand on their head to indicate wanting to comment on what's just been said, or they can put their elbow in the air to indicate they want to change the topic to something that's just occurred to them. When I ask students to indicate they have heard the most recent instruction, I always have them do something new:

"Wiggle the fingers on your left hand if you heard where you'll be putting the computers when you're done."

"Stick out your tongue if you understand the material enough to help another student."

"Stand up and sit down quickly if you have submitted the assignment already."

Maybe there are signs for agreement or disagreement. Have fun making up ways to communicate through movement.

6. **Kinesthetic Paragraph Writing.** One lesson I do when I teach the outline of a basic constructed response paragraph is to have the students represent the sentences themselves using sentence strips, tabletops, and chairs. I group the students into four to five kids per group. Then, the student who writes the main topic sentence on a sentence strip stands on a table holding their sentence. The next

> "I am engaged when we do things where we moving around. In history to show what it was like working in a factory during the Industrial revolution, our teacher made the room messy and pretend as if it was a factory (he made machine sounds through paper in the air as if a machine broke."
>
> —Fernando, Middle Schooler

Photo courtesy of Heather Wolpert-Gawron

Photo courtesy of Heather Wolpert-Gawron

student expands on this statement and sits on the table. The third student writes the evidence to support the main topic sentence and sits on a chair. The fourth writes commentary that aligns with the evidence and sits on the floor. Finally, the fifth student writes the conclusion sentence and reclines on the floor. If we read the sentence strips from top to bottom, you have a full paragraph. This is a technique that can embed paragraph structure into any subject area, whether teaching literary analysis or mathematical justifications.

7. **Create responsibilities that embrace those who need to move around.** If you know that you have a student who is continuously moving around, perhaps you can create responsibilities to utilize that. Rather than get frustrated that Richard got up to get water yet again, perhaps he's your go-to guy to hand out papers or retrieve supplies for your small groups. If you have a group that is looking tired, have them jump up, out-of-the-blue, and do a few jumping jacks. The oxygen to the brain will wake them up and the quality you get as a result will outweigh the short time supposedly wasted by having them do the activity.

The bottom line is that students need movement in order to focus. So while many teachers try to sit on the jumpiness, the leg bouncing, and the kids who continuously get up and move around, perhaps they should be embracing those tendencies instead.

ENGAGING TEACHER SPOTLIGHT

Here is a lesson from a wonderful language arts teacher, Elizabeth Harrington. Liz is an associate director of the University of California at Irvine Writing Project and a veteran middle school teacher.

OVERVIEW

This lesson focuses on using a kinesthetic learning strategy to scaffold the concept of theme, and the practice of writing commentary. Students "travel" around the room in small groups, visiting posters displaying significant quotes from the text. They discuss the significance of each quote, and write their comments on the posters. As the groups progress from one poster to the next, they also have the opportunity to add to the comments of previous groups.

Prior to the lesson described below, students had read the novel *Dragonwings* by Laurence Yep, and had responded to it in a variety of ways, including making dialectical journals, and participating in small group and whole-class discussions. During these discussions, we had touched upon several ideas connected to themes in the novel, without specifically referring to them as themes. This lesson was designed as a "mini-inquiry" to introduce them to the concept that a novel may have multiple themes, and to show that the themes in a novel are also connected to our everyday lives.

Note: This lesson is based upon strategies described in the book *Reading Non-Fiction* by Kylene Beers and Robert Probst (2016).

STEP-BY-STEP

1. I selected a number of quotes that relate to the ideas we had touched upon in class discussion. I typed the quotes in large font, cut them out, and glued them in the centers of construction paper posters, which I then placed at intervals

around the room, some on walls, and some on tables, as space permitted.

2. I divided the class into groups of three or four students, and stationed each group by a different poster.

3. Students had 3 minutes to read the quote on the poster, talk together about its significance to "real" life, not just to the situation in the novel, and add a comment by writing on the poster.

4. When the timer signaled the end of the 3-minute time period, each group moved on to the next poster, and the process was repeated. For the second and subsequent posters, the groups had the additional option of responding to another group's comment, as shown in Figures 4.1 and 4.2.

FIGURE 4.1

PAPER POSTER

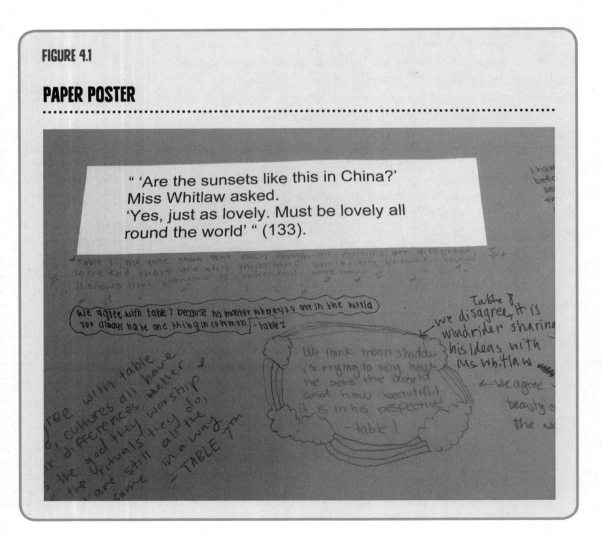

FIGURE 4.2

PAPER POSTER

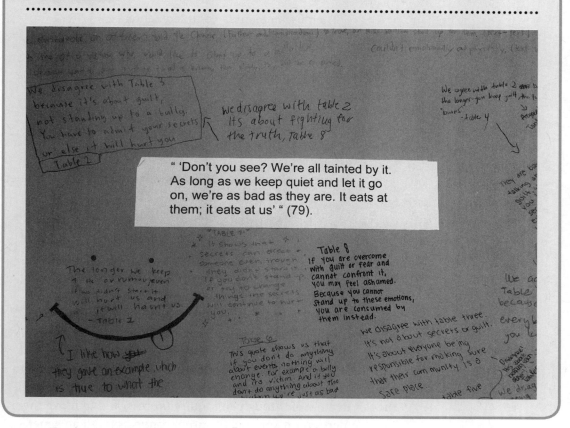

5. On the following day, after each group had responded to all of the quotes, the class did a "gallery walk," during which they walked around from poster to poster reading and discussing all of the comments written on the posters. At this time, they had the option of adding additional comments if they chose to do so.

6. There followed a whole-class discussion, during which I asked students to share any commonalities that they had noticed among the quotes as they examined them. This led to a discussion about themes in the novel.

7. Each group then selected one of the themes that had been identified, and created a poster that included the following information:

- Title and author

- Theme statement (a complete sentence)

- Three quotes, correctly cited, that clearly reflected the theme

- Analysis of each quote (commentary) that discussed how the quote related to the theme statement

- An "overall statement" discussing the theme's significance to life in general

The poster also included illustrations and a symbolic border.

8. Students later wrote a literary analysis essay on theme, and used the posters as resources.

REFLECTION

My initial goal for this activity was to have my students practice writing commentary that goes deeper than simply paraphrasing the quote, which is what most of them were doing in the dialectical journals they had made while reading the novel. I also wanted to scaffold their understanding of how to identify and articulate the themes in a novel through an inquiry process, and to move them to an understanding of how literature connects to life in general.

While my initial goals for the lesson series were met, I found that this activity had additional benefits that went beyond our study of *Dragonwings*. I was about to introduce them to the concept of blogging, and of commenting on blogs. The experience of commenting on the *Dragonwings* quotes, and on the comments of other students, paved the way for learning to make thoughtful and insightful comments on their peers' blogs.

My students really enjoyed this series of lessons. They were able to be out of their seats, and they had an opportunity to respond to the text in a way that was fun and engaging. As they progressed around the room, they became excited to see and respond to what others had written, as well as offering ideas of their own. Students were highly engaged throughout the process, and particularly enjoyed the gallery walk because they wanted to see what everyone else had written about "their" quote. The room was filled with energy and with conversations about literature.

DISCUSSION QUESTIONS

1. How can you use physical movement to symbolically represent a concept from your subject area?

2. How often can students move around your room to change their perspective of the classroom environment?

3. Would it benefit students to learn that increasing oxygenation to the brain increased learning capacity? How might you create a lesson that helped students embrace that fact?

4. Think of your favorite, albeit more traditionally crafted, lesson. How might you modify this beloved lesson to include more movement?

Photo courtesy of Davis Lester

CHAPTER FIVE

GIVE US CHOICES

"I like to have some choice in what I do."

OVERVIEW

In 1971, Starbucks opened in Pike Place Market in Seattle, Washington. Since then, according to recent math, Starbucks now offers up to 87,000 options for your sipping pleasure ("Starbucks Stay Mum on Drink Math," 2008).

OK, perhaps I'm creating a correlation here, but hear me out. It is a suspicious coincidence that during the first decade of Starbucks' life, there was also the birth of a large study in humanistic education by David N. Aspy and Flora N. Roebuck. This study spanned the 1970s and focused on student-centered learning, an element of which is student choice.

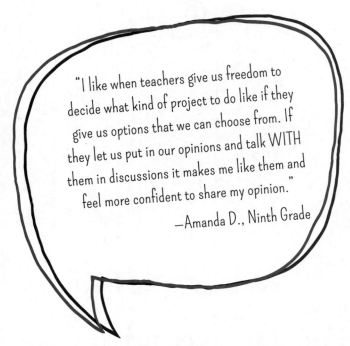

"I like when teachers give us freedom to decide what kind of project to do like if they give us options that we can choose from. If they let us put in our opinions and talk WITH them in discussions it makes me like them and feel more confident to share my opinion."

—Amanda D., Ninth Grade

Now, I'm not equating the import of weighing your options in caffeinated beverage with one's choice in how to display knowledge of your content area, but it seems to me that at some point, there was a shift in expectation in our culture outside of school that soon became reflected within school as well.

According to the student engagement survey, student choice is listed as one of the most engaging strategies a teacher can allow in the classroom. Want to know how to engage students, enthuse them, and bring out their best effort? Want ways to differentiate organically? Give them a voice in their decisions. In a society that barely listens to each other, listen to our students. In a system that can be a flood of top down, let your classroom be one that allows voices to trickle up. We have, in our very classrooms, the brains that will solve the problems of tomorrow, but to give them training means we have to give their neurons a chance to solve the problems of today.

"In a system that can be a flood of top down, let your classroom be one that allows voices to trickle up."

Student choice builds ownership in the learning.

Student choice allows students to display their learning in the way that they feel best represents their knowledge.

Student choice enforces true differentiation.

THE ACADEMIC BENEFITS OF STUDENT CHOICE

Jim Bentley (2016) of the Buck Institute of Education (BIE) is an expert in student choice since it is a deeply rooted element in project-based learning, the strategy at the heart of the Buck Institute. He believes that student choice also redefines the position of teacher from knowledge authority to learning guide. He says that

[e]ngagement is a fire that can quickly die out when things get challenging. That's where it's important to build in student

voice and choice as well as the concepts of sustained inquiry and critique and revision. With student voice and choice, teachers are managing the work of students not controlling it. If a student or team wants to take a certain angle on a task they can—given it aligns with the purpose of the project. . . . Students generally respond well, liking the freedom.

> "Something that engages me as a student are assignments where you get to have more choice. . . . I feel that choice definitely encourages more creativeness."
>
> —Patrice X., Sixth Grade

In fact, student choice is so important to BIE that it has included it in the rubric it uses to assess units of study to ensure that student choice is encouraged and utilized. The rubric itself promotes the belief that

Choice + Agency = Learning

It asks teachers to evaluate whether "Students have opportunities to express voice and choice on important matters (questions asked, texts and resources used, people to work with, products to be created, use of time, organization of tasks)" (Davis, 2016).

This ambiguity of student choice can intimidate any teacher, but is a surmountable fear and a fear that must be challenged. In terms of creating evidence of knowledge, the intense structure of "do this, like this" is not as effective as "what way would best work for you?"

And research backs up what the students have long known. Results from a 2010 study show that when

> "The thing that I would say makes learning better is when everyone has more freedom in what they choose, maybe in the topic of our research, or being able to choose to write, draw, or build something. I just think that at times when it is difficult for a student to express himself, and it frustrates them to have to bow down to the strict guidelines. I'm not syang let students do whatever they want, but perhaps more freedom in choosing will pipe mere curiosity, interest, and inner sparkly talent."
>
> —Thomas T., Eighth Grade

students received a choice of homework they reported higher intrinsic motivation to do homework, felt more competent regarding the homework, and performed better on the unit test compared with when they did not have a choice. In addition, a trend suggested that having choices enhanced homework completion rates compared with when no choices were given. (Patall, Cooper, & Wynn, 2010)

The theory of consuming information in a single, teacher-prescribed way, also may not play into the strengths of each and every student. The good news is that there is guidance out there to help teachers select the most appropriate elements of their teaching in which to offer choice.

In fact, research proves that student choice increases both engagement and motivation for tween, teens, and in fact, all age levels. According to Robert Marzano, "When given choice by teachers, students perceive classroom activities as more important. Choice in the classroom has also been linked to increases in student effort, task performance, and subsequent learning" (Marzano Research, n.d.). Marzano goes on to report that granting students choice directly aligns with student engagement. He encourages teachers to give choice in the following:

1. Tasks to perform

2. Ways to report

3. Establishing their own learning goals

This seems to promote more ownership in their learning and outcomes. Marzano further recommends the following:

To provide a choice of task to students, a teacher can provide multiple task options on an assessment and ask students to respond to the one that interests them most. Similarly, a teacher can provide students with the option to choose their own reporting format. The two most common reporting formats are written and oral reports. . . . However, students may also choose to present information through debates, video reports, demonstrations, or dramatic presentations. To give students a particularly powerful choice, a teacher can ask students to create their own learning goals. When giving students the option to design their own learning goals, a teacher should hold students accountable for both their self-identified learning goal as well as teacher-identified learning goals for that unit.

Allowing students some choice in their learning is clearly proving successful. In 2008, a meta-analysis was conducted by Patall, Cooper, and Robinson (n.d.) that examined 41 studies on the topic. "Results indicated that providing choice enhanced intrinsic motivation, effort, task performance, and perceived competence, among other outcomes," according to its authors.

> "I get engaged in creative assignments, that allow us to pick, and choose how we execute the finished product. In history, we were allowed to choose what our poster was about, as long as it related to history."
>
> —Riker G., High Schooler

But our goals for our students are not all academic. We need students to learn how to make decisions, how to weigh options, and how to advocate for their opinions. Therefore, if we are to help develop students into citizens, we need to include choice as a vital strategy toward that goal.

Alfie Kohn (2010) believes that

> [t]he psychological benefits of control are, if anything, even more pronounced. All else being equal, emotional adjustment is better over time for people who experience a sense of self-determination; by contrast, few things lead more reliably to depression and other forms of psychological distress than a feeling of helplessness. . . . The truth is that, if we want children to take responsibility for their own behavior, we must first *give* them responsibility, and plenty of it. *The way a child learns how to make decisions is by making decisions, not by following directions.*

School is a place to help train students to handle the choices that life throws at them; if anything, we should be encouraging as many opportunities as possible for students to work that muscle in the gym that is school.

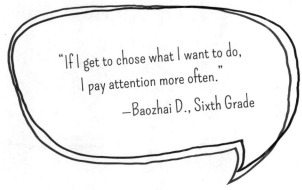

> "If I get to chose what I want to do, I pay attention more often."
>
> —Baozhai D., Sixth Grade

> "As a student, I always wanted to do things with partners and/or different people in the classroom. I am more interested in the lesson if we get to choose what we want to do. For example, the teacher can give us 4 choices and we can pick from there."
>
> —Valeria H.

KEEPING STRUCTURE WHILE GIVING FREEDOM

So do we let students have the run of every decision? Of course not. The key is to give choices, but provide guidance and limitations when doing so. After all, you can't just say, "Hey it's time for Genius Hour. Study whatever you want!" You have to help students make choices by providing good choices to choose from in a structured environment.

In 2010, ASCD reported on that same 2008 meta-analysis that there was a correlation

> "Every student has their own unique brain and consequently, different interests, academic achievement and learning styles than their peers. For example, some students may be engaged by assignments that involve art whereas other students may be reluctant to do such assignments. Teachers should understand the diversity of their students and create choices for their projects. . . . Of course, this does not mean that every single homework assignment for the school year has to come with a choice. It's understandable that some skills must be learned in a certain way despite a student's reluctance to learning it. In addition, teachers would most likely be significantly stressed out if they had to create choices for every given assignment. However, the availability of choices once in awhile will assure students that they are, in a sense, being thought about."
>
> —Grace L., Eighth Grade

between giving students choices and their intrinsic motivation for doing a task, their overall performance on the task, and their willingness to accept challenging tasks. However, the researchers also found diminishing returns when students had too many choices: Giving more than five options produced less benefit than offering just three to five. The researchers concluded that with student choice, "too much of a good thing may not be very good at all. (Goodwin, 2010)

But there isn't a magic number, a sweet spot, of how much or what to offer. The key is to keep it changing, to keep it fresh, and to maintain options.

All of this is related to the recent debate of competence versus compliance. Are we assessing students on what they know, or rather on strictly prescribed ways to prove they know it? Are we presenting information in ways that many students can comprehend, or are we evaluating students in their ability to comprehend based on a single method of information delivery?

Student choice allows for a teacher to assess knowledge without dictating how that student needs to show it. And the fact that a student gets to participate in elements of choice increases the chances that the work will get submitted at all.

> "The way a child learns how to make decisions is by making decisions, not by following directions."
>
> —Alfie Kohn

"Allowing students to have a bit more freedom in how they learn makes it enjoyable and more involved."

—Amber S., Ninth Grade

ENGAGE WITH THE CONTENT!

In the video to the right, you'll be introduced to Diane Tom, a seventh-grade science teacher who gives choice in her classroom in a variety of ways. As you watch her guide her students through a lesson about variables and the scientific method, think about what you are seeing as it relates to both student choice and the other chapters in this book. Think further on the following:

- What elements of choice does she give her students?
- How does she manage transitions in her classroom?
- How does Diane leverage open-ended questions to hand off the authority of learning to the students?

Video 5.1 Give Students Choice

WHAT GIVING STUDENTS CHOICE LOOKS LIKE IN THE CLASSROOM

Keeping in mind the prior research that proves there is such a thing as too much choice, it's important to just look at all the possible options that teachers have who are looking to incorporate more choice in their classrooms.

Options to offer choice:

1. **People to Work With.** Give students the chance to choose whether to work independently or with another student(s). As a teacher, you can still maintain some control by giving students input. Poll them to see the four students they would most want to work with and then give them the guarantee that at least one of those students will be working with them. Let's face it, life would be great if nobody got left out of the picking process or if every student felt welcomed in every group, but teachers might want to maintain some input here as well, if only to help students who socially need the push. Nevertheless, give students the ability to have some say in their coworkers. Don't you wish you could have some say in yours?

   "When I can choose my group I usually end up getting people that work well with me and we end up agreeing a lot more."
   —Peter C., Middle Schooler

2. **Resources to Use.** Guide students in how to research, but don't point them to every possible resource. Help foster independent learning by giving them the choice in what they are learning from.

   "I am most engaged when we do a project with groups that we can choose. Because Its more fun and makes me want to work harder."
   —Maria N., Eighth Grade

3. **Driving Questions.** In inquiry-based learning, students tend to develop their own questions that require research in order to form a solution. Being able to develop these questions, the questions that drive the learning, is not a small task, and can be used as their own informal assessment as

well. By allowing students to set the train on the track, you will have them buying into the learning throughout the journey.

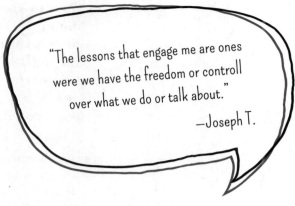

4. **Ways to Show Their Knowledge.** As Marzano said above, there are many ways in which a student can show what they know about the content area. From essays to dramatic interpretations, from digital slideshows to sculptures, from websites to podcasts, students can prove their knowledge and give evidence of their learning in an infinite number of ways.

5. **Which Rubric to Be Scored On.** Some teachers have taken to developing different rubrics that reflect different levels of understanding. In other words, if students feel they are ready, they can attach the advanced rubric to their essay or if they feel they aren't quite ready for that challenge, they can be assessed using a more standard or grade-level rubric. Rubrics can also be used to assess different elements of an assignment. Just imagine a student setting their own goals and then selecting the rubric to match that goal.

6. **What They Need to Work on to Improve/Learning Goals**. And speaking of setting goals, allow students to set their own goals and objectives. When I have my students begin the revision stage of essay writing, for instance, I always have them first state what they choose to have me look for in order to give more targeted feedback. In so doing, they not only show me that they are reflective and aware of the skill they need to work on, but they also pay closer attention to the feedback overall.

For instance, one student used the commenting tool in Google Drive to indicate what she wanted me to look for as I was reading her initial essay. She asked me the following:

Katie: How should I change my title to make it seem like a strong representation of the theme?

Student choice, therefore, helps me to help them.

7. **Ways to View and Record Assignments for Time Management.** Tweens and teens continue to need advice in how to manage their time, but they don't all connect with the same methods. Therefore, I give my students three different choices as ways to record their assignments or track their assignments. This is yet another way that choice feeds into our mission to differentiate.

   - Weekly: I post our classroom and homework online each week. On Mondays, students see what the upcoming week holds. This allows students to plan their workload and know when things are due in manageable pieces.

   - Daily: I break down each day on the board and let students know what we are doing throughout the period. Some students really can only take in bite-sized information at a time.

   - Quarter/Semester: I give students a rough timeline of what the quarter or semester looks like including key dates when larger assignments are due. Some students find this overwhelming, while others really like the overarching knowledge of what's to come.

8. **Scaffolds.** By the time students get to middle school, it's really vital that they have a choice in how they take notes or in what scaffolds to use. I'm not a fan of dictating what Thinking Map to use or if a student needs to use one at all. However, if they learned one earlier that they continue to rely on, why not allow them to use it? There might also be a different kind of graphic organizer that does help them. Perhaps a student likes using Cornell Notes, while others might prefer index cards or a digital program like Evernote. We can dictate that a brainstorming element needs to be included in the learning process, but we shouldn't be dictating for students the scaffold that works best for them.

9. **Text Structures**. Give students choice in the structure of their essays. We know that the traditional five-paragraph essay doesn't exist in the world outside of school, and in fact, in many of the formal tests administered to students, that standardized structure never even appears, so teach students to take risks with their written structure. Teach students how to organize their thoughts using subheadings, bullets, and numbering. Teach them how to use transitions that not only work between paragraphs, but also work

between sections of text. Teach them about captions and integrating quotes. Allow students to embed images and videos into their essays as well as data or textual evidence. Give them choice in the structure of their essay, and you might just find that they can communicate their knowledge more clearly than trying to fit what's in the brain into a structure that doesn't connect with them.

10. **Choice of opinion/prompts, etc.** Give students options of prompts to respond to and/or create open-ended questions that can only be answered by each individual student. By giving them leeway to decide on their own opinions or choose from a list of content-related prompts, you will find that their excitement for responding increases. And if their engagement increases, you will get the highest level of response they can muster.

11. **Seating.** Choice of seating was actually mentioned a number of times in our student engagement survey. In my classroom, for instance, I have beanbag chairs, standing desks with bar stools, video game chairs, small group tables, and plenty of carpet. Different kids like to work

FLEXIBLE SEATING

Photo courtesy of Heather Wolpert-Gawron

Photo courtesy of Heather Wolpert-Gawron

in different positions. Some like to work under tables or facing walls. I call them "cave dwellers." Others like to stand at the taller tables, dismissing chairs altogether. Others like to sit, back-to-back, on the floor. (See photos.) I also find that they tend to make wise choices. More hyper kids, for instance, will work quantitatively more while rocking in a video game chair than seated static at a desk. The only drawback is that it took me longer to memorize the names because they also liked to try different views of the classroom and different seating options, particularly at the beginning of the year. But (shrug) that was my problem. When we're talking about engagement, it's a no-brainer.

12. **Deadlines.** You know how you get slammed when all those essays or projects come in all at once? Why not avoid that dilemma and allow students to select the deadlines themselves? Once I have introduced a long-term assignment, I generally open up a window of dates for students to choose from. I send out a Google Form that allows students to select from a drop-down menu of choices. Their selection then seeds a spreadsheet automatically that I can sort by date. The date they select is their firm deadline. So I'm still honoring the assessment of responsibility, but I am also honoring the process of bringing students into the decision-making process.

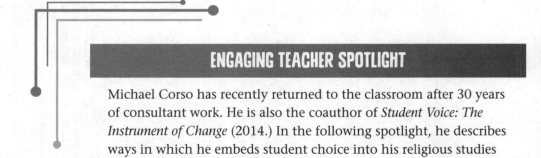

ENGAGING TEACHER SPOTLIGHT

Michael Corso has recently returned to the classroom after 30 years of consultant work. He is also the coauthor of *Student Voice: The Instrument of Change* (2014.) In the following spotlight, he describes ways in which he embeds student choice into his religious studies lessons.

OVERVIEW

I teach a World Religions course to high school seniors at Catholic Memorial School in Boston, Massachusetts. As you can imagine, students vary in their interest in their own religion and that of their families', so I felt I needed a strategy that would engage students in a different way. There was little likelihood students would do more than go through the motions of learning about various world religions if I used traditional, "sage on the stage," pedagogical strategies. From working on Student Voice for so many years, I knew that student engagement is heightened when students teach and learn from one another.

For this reason, I created a process and a culminating project that permitted as much student input as possible. The overall goal was to develop a class-length presentation (slideshow) and write a five-page paper on a chosen religion.

I think the key to success with a strategy like this is to provide the maximum amount of freedom and choice possible within a rubric and framework that is as clearly articulated as possible. While as the teacher I had created clear guidelines, students were able to choose the following:

- To work in partnership or not
- Their topic of study
- The resources used
- Their interviewee
- What particular aspects of the religion to study and include
- How to craft their slide deck
- How to assess a peer
- How to assess himself

STEP-BY-STEP

1. After I facilitated learning about the importance of interreligious dialogue, especially given many of the issues in our world, we divided the religions we had to study among the students. Students could choose the religion they wanted to work on.

2. Students also decided if they wanted to work with a partner (for some this also heightens engagement) or on their own. If working with a partner, research and presentation had to be done together, but the paper was required to be an independent exercise. I made clear that while I expected overlap in the papers of a partnership, I also expect to see evidence of independent reflection and articulation.

3. Students were given guidelines for their research, presentation, and paper. For research, students could choose at least two other sources. Only one of these was a Web source, while the other was a print book. Students had to also choose someone to interview, a person who practices the religion they were studying. The highlight of nearly every presentation—and I think of the experience for each student in general—was the interview. Students at first expressed reservations about this requirement ("I don't know any Buddhists!"). I provided them with a number of strategies for locating an interviewee ranging from "ask your parents" to websites and Web searches to local interreligious agencies. No student required extra help locating someone after that and no student failed to interview someone. The presentation deck only guided students in terms of length and loose advice. Their slide deck presentation should contain a minimum of 10 slides. . . . Better presentations use images and not just texts on the slides. From there on in, students were permitted to choose how to develop the slides themselves.

4. As part of our preparation, we had read an excerpt from C. S. Lewis' *Mere Christianity* that used the analogy of a map to describe the importance of religion. I created a rubric that used the acronym "MAPPED" on which students assessed each other and themselves by choosing where their research and presentation fell on the chart. Their grade ended up being an average of the peer assessments, the student's self-assessment, and my own assessment. There was, therefore, an element of choice in how they assessed each other and themselves. When evaluating presentations, students were encouraged to write notes along with a score in each box. These were collected at the end of each presentation for safe keeping and redistributing for the next presentation. A student's classroom participation grade for that day was based on their meaningful approach to the evaluation of his or her peer.

Both structure and freedom are required to "jazz up" pedagogy because, like jazz, meaningful engagement is the result of careful arrangement (choices of how to assess on the rubric, choices in what resources to use, whom to interview, and what topic to study) like those highlighted above. And as a teacher, hearing students say, as they leave a class in which a fellow student presented, "That was cool" is music to my ears.

DISCUSSION QUESTIONS

1. Think of the ways in which you might organize a cause-and-effect essay. What are three different graphic organizers that might help you scaffold this kind of essay? Which would you choose and why? What are the benefits of the other two you did not choose to use?

2. Let's pretend that you have assigned students to do a book study on a biography about someone famous in your field of study. What are five different methods you can offer students to demonstrate the contributions this person made to their content area? Make sure each of these artifacts represent different strategies of output (i.e., a screencast, a dramatic reenactment, an infographic, etc.).

3. What are the challenges a teacher faces when allowing students to choose whom they get to work with? How might you frontload or proactively tackle those challenges so that you do not disallow students the choice?

4. Think of your favorite, albeit more traditionally crafted, lesson. How might you modify this beloved lesson to include student choice?

Photo courtesy of Davis Lester

CHAPTER SIX

SHOW US YOU'RE HUMAN TOO

"I love when my teachers are excited!"

OVERVIEW

We all know how vital school can be; but unfortunately, sometimes we misinterpret the need to convey importance with the need to convey solemnity. Sure, we know school plays a critical role as a student's "brain gym," a place where, for years, young persons can "work out" their understanding of both their place in the world and how their knowledge can play a key part in changing that world. Yet despite its importance, school doesn't have to be a place where teachers have to adopt a colder, more academic facade. Throughout our student engagement survey, students overwhelmingly mentioned that what engaged them the most was when the teacher was also unabashedly engaged, honest with their own foibles, and could also have a good laugh. In other words, students wanted their teachers to be more, well, human.

Just because the primary role of school is academic doesn't mean it has to be so serious. And students appreciate when teachers throw out all aloofness and bring their smiles and enjoyment to the table. They want to see that the teacher has enthusiasm for both their subject and their students, and they had very specific advice for how to show that enthusiasm. The student engagement survey was peppered over and over again with students who begged for the following:

- See their teacher's own enthusiasm for the subject they were assigned to teach
- Feel that the teacher really cared for them and their learning
- Laugh with their teachers about their content
- Hear personal stories from teachers as they related to their lessons
- Learn about times when their own teachers failed, only to get back up again

What students were really asking for, although not explicitly stated, was to humanize the authority figure in the room. They wanted to see teachers laugh, open up, share what made them love learning, and share their struggles as they learned.

It can be scary to open up to anybody, and asking teachers to drop some of the wall between themselves and their students is bound to cause some fear. But the survey tells us that in doing so, students will respond.

UNABASHEDLY SHOW THAT YOU CARE ABOUT THE CONTENT

We've all been in classrooms where the teacher seemed unenthusiastic about what he or she was actually teaching.

"[S]tudents appreciate when a teacher throws out all aloofness and brings their smiles and enjoyment to the table."

Perhaps that teacher just didn't realize their own expressions—facial, physical, vocal—played a large part in how engaged their students were in the subject.

But before we talk about how to develop enthusiasm for the content, we need to unpack a little of what might be going on to contribute to an unenthusiastic teacher.

For one thing, some of this lack of enthusiasm isn't the fault of the teachers themselves. There are far too many teachers set up for failure in this area because they are tasked with teaching out of their area of expertise, or in fact, at times, out of their area of interest. How difficult it must be to muster up enthusiasm for a subject in which you hold little knowledge or for a subject that does not excite you! It's important to note here that according to a survey conducted by the National Center for Educational Statistics, almost 2% of over 600,000 teachers reported in 2011 that they were ill prepared to teach in their assigned subject area (National Centre for Education Statistic, n.d.). That's approximately 12,000 teachers!

And this isn't merely an issue in America either. A 2015 survey from the Australian Council for Educational Research reported that 40% of seventh- to tenth-grade students were taught by an out-of-field mathematics teacher.

In England, the *Independent* reports that a 2016 survey of 885 schools "reveals 73 percent were having to put teachers not trained in the subject they were teaching in front of classes" (Garner, 2016). Nevertheless, a teacher must combat these circumstances and continue to model enthusiasm in teaching.

> "When the teacher has a deep passion for the subject, you do feel as if you want to get involved too. I won't mention any names, but I do have a teacher who has a deep passion for what she does. She is always thinking about it and knows a lot about the stuff she teaches. So, when I see her skipping (literally) around the classroom when we are learning about the Medieval Times, I feel as if the learning material is pretty good and that I want to try and see what's so good about it. So, it is natural for me to get excited as well."
>
> —Kelli O., Seventh Grade

"There are far too many teachers set up for failure in this area because they are tasked with teaching out of their area of expertise. . . . Nevertheless, a teacher must combat these circumstances, and continue to model enthusiasm in teaching."

"I also love when my teachers are excited. Sometimes it makes them seem a little geeky, but it makes it much more fun. (Sometimes we want to find out what there is to be so excited about.). . . . Students respect that."

—Deke G., Twelfth Grade

"The stuff that engages me is how enthusiastic the staff/teachers are. . . . When the teachers raise their voice and get exited, I turn my head and say 'Wow, what you're going to say must be interesting.'"

—Hayden P., Seventh Grade

The key is to absolutely, unabashedly show enthusiasm for your subject matter. This not only creates a more engaging style of teaching, but it actually contributes to building a community of comfort within the classroom itself. In other words, "geek out." The teacher has to model enthusiasm in the classroom, to an uber nerdy level, in order to allow students the feeling that they too can shed their masks. When I talk to teachers about this, I always refer them to this great quote from actor/writer/director Simon Pegg (n.d.) (from *Shawn of the Dead* and *Star Trek* fame):

Being a geek is all about being honest about what you enjoy and not being afraid to demonstrate that affection. It means never having to play it cool about how much you like something. It's basically a license to proudly emote on a somewhat childish level rather than behave like a supposed adult. Being a geek is extremely liberating.

In fact, I'm not the only one using this quote in their teaching. Trevor Hershberger, a gifted young high school teacher and fellow of the National Writing Project featured earlier in this book, says the following:

I start the year off with my sophomores by introducing them to Simon Pegg's remark. Then I ask them to share with me in writing what they are a geek about, whether it's sci-fi, metal rock bands, or football. I take this liberating mentality to heart in my classroom on a regular basis. I share my affection for bands by performing holiday songs on my saxophone in December. I wear my geeky enthusiasm for Shakespeare and musical theater on my sleeve by introducing a unit on Hamlet with a song from the musical Something Rotten. I shamelessly demonstrate my love of Disneyana by relating just about any concept to a Disney movie and doing things like teaching symbol analysis via the video clip of "Just Around the Riverbend" from Pocahontas. And all of these examples are ways that I bring my passion for music into my classroom every day.

Trevor's quote brings up an important delineation between what "geek" used to represent and what it has now become. While being a geek used to mean that you were only into comic books and science, the new definition is broader, and that can be leveraged to benefit your students' learning. It's vital for the good of your classroom community—and, ultimately, for the achievement of your students—to let those kids know that your room is a safe harbor for their geekdom, whatever it may be. It shows you care about your material and their interests as well.

But what does "enthusiasm" look like? Silly question for many, perhaps, but for others, awareness of facial expression and posture goes a long way. I know this sounds a little micromanaging, but it's important to point out that I was a speech and debate coach for 12 years, so when I was thinking about how to show enthusiasm for one's content, I thought I'd break it down into muscle groups: literally.

The fact is that some people, even those who have already become successful adults, struggle to emote. Nevertheless, emoting is clearly important to students.

This may seem silly, but let's break down the four basic quadrants on the body to review how our emotions are displayed and interpreted. By the way, this review works for students too:

> "It depends how energetic and live they are, enthusiastic teachers can make you focus on things better, even if its about something you dont like."
> — Wayde W., Twelfth Grade

> "I enjoy learning in an enthusiastic environment. If the teacher is passionate, excited . . . then I will cooperate and retain the information."
> —Jennifer B., Twelfth Grade

> "[Y]our room is a safe harbor for their geekdom, whatever it may be."

> "Teachers shouldn't be completely dead paned."
> —Madison, Eighth Grade

1. Face: Learn how to control your eyebrows and your lower lids. Does your smile reach your eyes? Can you look in the mirror and show excitement and surprise? Learn what muscles control your facial expressions by touching the area you most want to trigger and exercise that muscle into movement over and over again. My dad did this when he was a teenager and wanted to learn how to raise a single eyebrow like Errol Flynn to impress a girl.

2. Spine/Posture: Are you standing up straight or slumping in the classroom? I'm not saying you have to have military-grade posture, but keep in mind that how you stand sometimes is interpreted as interested or disinterested.

3. Arms: Do you use them to express yourself, or do you tend to keep them by your side or crossed in front of you? Do they form a barrier between you and the students?

4. Legs: Are you standing on your hip, leaning against furniture while you talk? Do you do the rock-n-roll when you speak or do you sway a bit? Are you a leg bouncer? What we do with our legs can say a lot about our own nervousness and can be misread as a lack of desire to be doing what you are doing.

Check out the screenshots from some of this book's video package. If you watch the videos themselves, you will notice that these teachers all differ in style and delivery. Nevertheless, they don't lack an ability to emote.

EMBARRASSING (BUT NECESSARY) FACIAL EXPRESSIONS

Photo courtesy of Davis Lester

Photo courtesy of Davis Lester

Photo courtesy of Davis Lester

Look, none of these methods are meant to dictate false engagement or choreograph that which you don't internalize, but it's important to know how posture and expressions can be read, and what you can do to send the messages you want to send.

After all, when you model unabashed enthusiasm for your subject area (or any topic), you'll be amazed at what you learn about your own students.

"Emotion. I love it when teachers actually have some emotion when they're talking, giving a lesson, etc. Maybe when they're excited, they actually show some excitement, not just talking in monotone. I'm sure everyone has experienced this before. You're in a room and there's a presenter. The person just talks with no emotion whatsoever. It's almost like a six page essay without dialogue. You can get lost and it might get uninteresting."

—Irene, Middle Schooler

UNABASHEDLY SHOW THAT
YOU CARE ABOUT THE STUDENTS

We've all been in classrooms where it was cut-and-dry content delivery with little thought about the students as individuals. Perhaps the teacher felt rushed and the effort of warmth was abandoned. Perhaps the philosophy of the teacher was that the relationship between teacher and student should be one that did not extend beyond content deliverer and content receiver. Regardless, if a teacher really wants to engage kids, they have to care about what their students feel and experience beyond the classroom.

By creating a classroom environment that allows for geeking out, I have in the past learned a lot about my students because they were also eager to share. I learned that David, the skateboarder who was suspended for tagging the school over the weekend, really longed to go to culinary school. As a result, we talked Top Chef nonstop for an entire school year. I learned that Melanie spoke four languages, and that she wanted to use her facility with language to work with the United Nations. I learned that Eduardo did the crossword puzzle with his abuela every Sunday morning, and despite the laughs he got when he first admitted it, he became the go-to guy to have on the classroom Jeopardy team.

In fact, by sharing your enthusiasm with your students, you might find similarities between you, and that too can bring out more engagement in your classroom. In the study, "Creating Birds of Similar Feathers: Leveraging Similarity to Improve

> "As a student I really appreciate when teachers pay attention to my needs. Like if Im having trouble with a certain unit or assignment, i appreciate it when my teachers take the time to actually help me out. Also teachers should demonstrate patience if they want to engage students. . . . Getting to know the students can be an effective method as well, this allows students to trust teachers."
>
> —Mohamed L., Twelfth Grade

> "Teachers who care about us, techers who teach with a smile and enthusiasm . . ."
>
> —Ethan A., Tenth Grade

Teacher Student Relationships and Academic Achievement," the authors state the following:

Many studies have shown that students with better TSRs [Teacher Student Relationships] tend to achieve more highly in school . . . have more positive attitudes toward school and their subject matter . . . [and] students more willingly pay attention in class when they think their teacher cares more. On the other hand, adolescents who perceived more disinterest and/or criticism from their teachers were more likely to cause discipline problems. (Gehlbach et al., In press)

So, it's important that teachers recognize this vital relationship between themselves and their students. This partnership only comes with caring about the children as well as the material. In fact, according to the National Educational Association (n.d.),

Most teachers care about imparting knowledge to students. But the best teachers also care about the relational aspect of teaching. They take time to establish a trusting and caring connection with their students, who in turn become more receptive to what's being taught.

In other words, the care you show in the classroom must extend beyond enthusiasm for both teaching and the subject itself; it must also include enthusiasm about working with your young clients. Create a classroom culture that celebrates geekdom, and you'll be advancing tolerance, empathy, and — yes — achievement.

"Make a connection to a single student, not just a whole class. Figure out the student. . . . Become a supporter and mentor that we as humans can learn from."
—Eliza P., Eighth Grade

"[O]ne thing that really engages me is having teachers that will be there for you whenever you need them. Having teachers that will help me and make me grow as a student in each subject makes me want to come to school to learn."
—Aiden, Tenth Grade

"I like it when the teacher enjoys the presence of the kids."
—Eduardo M., Eighth Grade

In a recent study of almost 400 students and their 25 teachers published in the *Journal of Educational Psychology*, the control groups of teachers and students were given information about five similarities they shared. Merely knowing about those similarities was praised as helping to increase their relationships. The abstract of the study, written by Todd Rogers (2017), reports that these similarities help promote relationships in particular "between teachers and their 'underserved' students." As a result, "This brief intervention appears to close the achievement gap at this school by over 60%."

Indeed, in study after study, we find a correlation between caring for the students beyond being mere academic receivers of information and student achievement. According to a 2008 study by Richard M. Muller,

> Research has indicated that students need to feel that their teachers care about them, want the best for them, and are invested in their success before students will give their full effort . . . student and teacher perceptions support the findings that the highest achieving schools combine an emphasis on academics with a culture of caring that reflect higher rates of pro-social behaviors and lower rates of antisocial behaviors among students. Further, school differences favoring more positive perceptions of teacher caring and commitment have corresponded to higher rates of academic achievement in those schools.

"What engages me are teachers who do not just passionately teach students, but mentor them to become better people."
—Bao-Zhi Y., Twelfth Grade

"Another thing that engages me as a middle school student are positive and encouraging teachers that tell me what is wrong with my work and who also focus on what I have done right. In my perspective, having a teacher that believes in me shows me that I have the potential to succeed."
—Denise, Seventh Grade

Showing enthusiasm for our students, their lives, and their efforts can be as simple as using appropriate praise. It's not about giving out false praise simply to generate student confidence. They can see that from a mile away. I'm talking about concrete, accurate, and honest praise when it's deserved.

Teachers' enthusiasm clearly makes a difference. What this means is that while a tween or teen might appear to push away adults during this time of life, the fact remains that these students can still acknowledge that they thrive more knowing our support is present and constant. These students feel they are more engaged in school and learning when the adults are more engaged in them.

THE POWER OF HUMOR IN THE CLASSROOM

One of the ways that teachers can show their humanity is by bringing humor to the classroom. I'm clearly not talking about jokes with questionable humor or grossness to go for the cheap laugh. I'm talking about seeing the humor around you, about tapping into levity in the classroom in a way that can make a kid smile during one of the most challenging, and sometimes darkest times, in a person's life. Being a teenager is hard; making a teenager smile is priceless.

So we don't want to use humor that falls flat or is offensive, and many teachers spurn using humor because they are fearful it will do just that. But we also know that laughter in the classroom wakes up the brain and can make students excited to be in our classrooms day in and day out. In particular, students seemed to relate to teachers who are also able to laugh at themselves.

"I hate disappointing my teachers especially if they try so hard to make me the best that I can be . . . I am not the perfect student but having my teacher want to work with me makes me feel special and like I can do it. . . . The greatest teachers believe in you when you don't believe in yourself."

– Amanda, Eighth Grade

"In all honesty, what helped to engage me as a student was the fact that a teacher actually showed me that they cared about what we had to say."

–Veronica D., Tenth Grade

"Being a teenager is hard; making a teenager smile is priceless."

"I tend to be engaged in learning more when the teacher is funny and kind of loud."

–Rochelle C., A Junior High Student

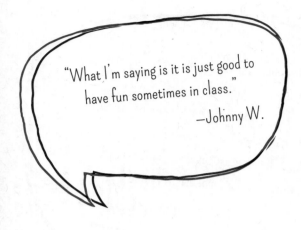

"What I'm saying is it is just good to have fun sometimes in class."

—Johnny W.

I also understand the fear many teachers have that somehow, if we buy into using humor, we'll need to entertain our students at all times. Some believe that we'll be contributing to a generation of students who require teachers to do a soft-shoe just to get students to want to learn. Of course, this isn't the case. Nevertheless, we aren't only in the business of understanding our own content; we're in the business of using strategies that best communicate that content, and our "clients" clearly feel that there needs to be some lightheartedness in the classroom that is appropriate for their grade level. School simply doesn't need to be so gosh darn serious all the time.

"Some believe that we'll be contributing to a generation of students who require teachers to do a soft-shoe just to get students to want to learn. Of course, this isn't the case."

Interestingly, the use of humor to improve engagement can be quantified. According to a 2005 article published in *Teaching of Psychology*, psychology professors Mark Shatz and Frank LoSchiavo found that when teachers utilized humor directed at themselves to prove a point or shared items like content-related cartoons into their online introductory psychology course, their students, according to the American Psychology Foundation, logged on more often to the learning management system Blackboard. Zak Stambor (2006) of the APF reported that Shatz insists "Professors' jobs are to educate, not to entertain. . . . But if humor can make the learning process more enjoyable, then I think everybody benefits as a result."

"A teacher who is real and not afraid to speak their mind really gets my attention. . . . Humor is the light of life and that's how I like to learn."

—Hannah Y., Eleventh Grade

According to educator and author Mary Kay Morrison (2008), tapping into humor in the classroom does the following:

- Helps to create comfort
- Fires up the brain
- Brings content to life

In fact, in her research of brain scans, Morrison (2008) learned that there was great stimulation and activation going on in multiple locations of the brain when humor was utilized. As she shared in her book, *Using Humor to Maximize Learning*,

We're finding humor actually lights up more of the brain than many other functions in a classroom. . . . In other words, if you're listening just auditorily in a classroom, one small part of the brain lights up, but humor maximizes learning and strengthens memories.

Let's examine what exactly gets stimulated as we follow what happens to a tween and teen's brain when a joke journeys from the ear and into the brain.

OK, so let's say that the student is sitting in math class, and Mrs. X has just said something uproariously funny (or simply remotely humorous) that was related to her tenth-grade curriculum.

"I have a teacher that really engages me, is very funny, and make lessons so that you learn but you don't notice because he is funny. (Note: That subject was language arts, which I hate.)"

—Moses H., Middle Schooler

FIGURE 6.1

A JOKE'S JOURNEY

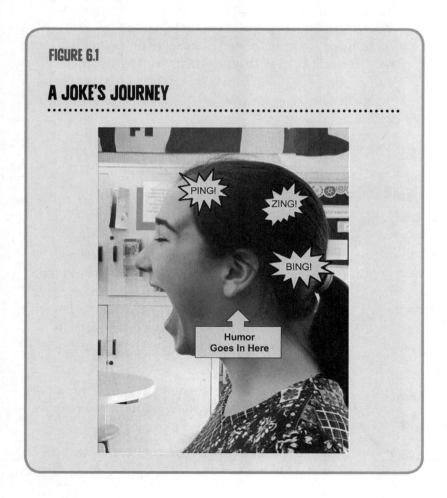

The teacher sends it out of her mouth and into the ears of her captive audience. That wee bit of an auditory powerhouse enters the brain and, like a pinball machine, the joke lights up multiple regions of the brain from the—*ping!*—frontal lobe (which processes received information) to the—*bing!*—supplementary motor area (that helps us learn information) to the—*pong!*—areas associated with our motor activities (based on the movements we make when we laugh) to the—*zing!*—nucleus accumbens (the regions used to process pleasure).

> "Jokes wake everyone up."
> —Noemi G., High Schooler

According to Carl Marci (2010), an assistant professor of psychiatry at Harvard Medical School and the director of social neuroscience in the Psychotherapy Research Program at Massachusetts General Hospital,

> When the punch line hits home, your heart rate rises, you jiggle with mirth, and your brain releases "feel good" neurotransmitters: dopamine, serotonin, and an array of endorphins. . . . The body sends a signal to the brain that says, "Hey, that's clever, that's worth it," and we laugh.

The "it" that's worth laughing for can therefore be connected to the curriculum content itself.

Laughter. Powerful stuff.

USING PERSONAL STORIES AS A TOOL FOR ENGAGEMENT

Another powerful way to show your humanity is to share your own personal stories and personal journey to highlight key points in your lessons. Of course, we don't want our personalities to overshadow our pedagogy; but we also know from the survey that many students respond when they hear about the personal side of their teachers.

> "It goes a long way when the teachers stay on topic but are still enthusiastic and funny."
> —Gavin F., Middle Schooler

Nevertheless, while storytelling is great, it must tie into our content. The stories must have a purpose, and students know the difference.

Students also want to know about their teachers, be it in a humorous way or not. This includes bringing our lives into the classroom to help support the curriculum. Our stories, our backgrounds, and our friends and family can become some of the supplemental material. For instance, when I teach my Superhero Unit, one that begins with writing a research-based science-fiction origin story, I have my friend from Caltech come in, quantum physicist Dr. Spyridon Michalakis, to help the students with their research. He is a fellow superhero-loving geek, and he was also the consultant on the movie *Ant-Man*. Not only does he help the students with the science I don't know, but he makes me look super cool in their eyes!

Bringing your life into the classroom and relating it to the curriculum not only wakes up the student and engages them, but it also models how higher-level thinkers make connections to the material. It contextualizes the content, while humanizing the learning process.

"Our stories, our backgrounds, and our friends and family can become some of the supplemental material."

The student engagement survey results were rich with comments and suggestions from students along these lines.

Storytelling doesn't have to take up your class period; it's about letting the students into facts about your own life and caring enough to ask about theirs.

For example, after I find out which students I will have in the fall, I send out an assignment asking them to email me over the summer and let them know what they're doing and how they are. Sure, this is my first informal way of seeing their writing quality, but it's also a way for me to respond individually to each student during a time when I have time to do so. It also gives me the chance to share a little of our commonalities if I can see the opportunity to tap into that.

One time, a student wrote to me that they went to DC in the summer and that they also spent time working on their swimming at the local pool. I responded,

"Know when to be strict, but not too strict, and be funny. Kids love that. I have had a few good teachers that have taught me important lessons, not only writing and reading lessons but lessons on how to live life, and I think at the age we are in that would help a lot. This doesn't mean to go all wise, just help your studnets as much as possible, even if what you are helping them on is not a school related topic. Give them that little extra push. (Some students need a good and firm shove)!"

—Tais, Ninth Grade

Summer Time Response!   — ⤢ ✕

Recipients

Summer Time Response!

Thanks so much for your email. It had such great written voice; I could really hear your personality as I was reading it.

I also went to DC this summer and I was blown away by the history all around me. My son has been singing the soundtrack to "Hamilton" all summer long, and seeing the places where so many events took place really brought it all home to him, you know?

Do you know that show?

On another note, I love swimming too. Once I was in high school my love of swimming also translated into scuba diving classes. Is that something you've ever thought about, or do you primarily like competitive swimming? Maybe you just love lounging around safely in a pool? Anyway, my point is, I love swimming too. True story: I was so into swimming as a child, that I sewed my jeans' legs together to pretend I was a mermaid, jumped into the pool, and sunk! Yeah. I don't recommend it.

Take care, and see you at the start of the school year!

> "I like when teachers really explain stuff and tell stories about what happened to help us understand it more."
>
> —Lauren N.

Using stories from your own life, or using your own interests to help engage students, also serves a different purpose. It helps to introduce students to sagas, experiences, and lessons learned that they might not otherwise be exposed to.

For instance, when my students come into my classroom, you never know the music that I might be playing. The music might be used to help teach the tone of the book we're reading or the concept we'll be studying. It could be college acapella's Tufts Beelzebubs. It could be a Danny Elfman score like that of *Batman* or *Beetlejuice*. It could be the opening of Lin Manuel-Miranda's *Hamilton* or even Gilbert and Sullivan's *I Am the Very Model of a Modern Major General*. They've done quickwrites of how they felt during the songs, or looked at the lyrics from songs and connected themselves to the material.

To teach similes, I've shared the story of when I jumped out of a plane, of how my teeth felt like they wore socks at the end of the leap from the dirt during the fall, and how the air pressure is so great it felt like I was laying belly-down on a table before we pulled the chute. I've also mentioned that I seem to remember trying to back out, because I recall that when I looked down from the plane's open door, I yelled,

"Heck no!" before being politely pushed out. They've then selected their own memories and used similes, metaphors, and hyperboles to describe their own events.

Here is an amazing example of how one teacher tapped into her own interests to bring more passion to her content area. Diane Tom is a middle school science as well as a teacher ranger for the National Parks Service (NPS). Her national parks project-based-learning unit is highlighted in Chapter 4 of this book. To help students in their research for this unit, she tapped her own network of friends.

Diane says the following:

> Informal surveys of my students confirmed what Richard Louv wrote about in his book *Last Child in the Woods*—a majority of my students are suffering from nature-deficit disorder. Most have had no personal experience with our amazing national parks. Since I have a network of colleagues in the NPS, the ideal circumstances existed to pull everything together to teach ecology science standards. . . . Initially, students researched national parks on the Internet and interviewed one of my park ranger friends through Skype. They asked questions related to the challenges and struggles of our national parks and what possible solutions were already being put in place. My personal connection with the NPS and my network of friends enabled me to creatively tap into park resources to plan a unique learning and life experience for my students.

"What engages me as a student in a classroom is teachers that can tell stories that relate to the topic/lesson . . . . There is some downfalls such as some teachers can't or don't have the ability to tell a story about themselves that relates to the topic, and the teachers that just tells about their life without really connecting to the topic or anything . . . and can make me more distracted to the lesson . . . but in my opinion, teachers that act like actual humans, interact with the students and share their ups and downs with each other, is the greatest way to engage a student in a lesson."

—Caleb D.

Students learn from us, and how we model our own humanity. Students learn from the grown-ups around them, and we, the educators, are around them more than any other adult, for at least 7 waking hours a day, for 180 days of the year.

BEING FALLIBLE TO HELP
STUDENTS UNDERSTAND LEARNING

Included in the stories I've shared with my students are the tales of my own failures, stories that related times when I fell, times when I got back up, and times when I fell again. I've shared about times when I was rejected or times when I disappointed myself. I've shared about the things I recovered from and even those I'm still, years later, gearing up the strength and courage to try again. We're running a marathon, not a sprint, and our decisions can reverberate for years.

We've all been talking about teaching this growth mindset, this ability to learn from mistakes. But arguably the most impactful strategy to teach growth mindset is in sharing and modeling it yourself. Allow your own vulnerabilities to be a part of the classroom material. Encourage your students to learn from their failures and trigger that learning by embracing your own.

> "My math class always engages me because my teacher shares the mistakes he makes throughout his life."
>
> —Tommy D., Seventh Grade

By doing so, it opens up the classroom community to learn more comfortably from criticism and critique.

Jim Bentley, teacher and National Faculty Member for the Buck Institute for Education, the leader in research for project-based learning, says the following about learning from criticism:

> Critique and revision is another way to keep the engagement alive. When a student attempts a task or tries to answer a question and comes up short, a PBL classroom doesn't treat that as an end, but rather a start. Andrew Miller, BIE National Faculty and ASCD author describes in his book *Freedom to Fail: How Do I Foster Risk Taking and Innovation in My Classroom?* the process of setting up students for controlled, incremental opportunities to "fail forward." In our classroom "fail" stands for "First attempt in learning"—something I borrowed from Andrew's book. . . . Most students have been conditioned to believe that when they get something wrong or struggle, they themselves are a failure. A PBL classroom looks at struggle as the beginning of learning. A great video we use in BIE trainings to show the power of feedback and

revision is by Ron Berger. The video, *Austin's Butterfly*, shows the power of kind, specific, and helpful feedback. Too many times students receive "feedback" In the form of a summative "grade." Feedback and grades are not synonymous yet too many teachers confuse the two, and too many students have been conditioned to attempt something and then release control and place their work in the hands of a teacher who passes judgment.

(You can view *Austin's Butterfly* by going to the companion website at http://resources.corwin.com/justaskus.)

Passing judgment needs to be recycled into a more productive process, one of giving feedback instead, so that we can help students develop that healthier growth mindset. And this begins with our own admissions of being human.

ENGAGE WITH THE CONTENT

The video to the right bottles up much of what we discovered in classrooms and with students as we looked through the lens of growth mindset. Check out how one math classroom celebrates how students reflect on their growth and hear from a number of students as well as they discuss their own failures. Watch the video and think about the following:

- How comfortable are you in sharing what challenges you the most?

- How can you help students who collapse before they even fail?

- How can you help students who don't take risks because of their fear?

- What are healthy attitudes/strategies that students who feel comfortable "getting back up again" possess?

Video 6.1 Share Your Own Humanity

Admitting we are fallible is vital because it helps model a passion to continue learning. If we can create an environment that is comfortable with failure and celebrates the effort of getting up to try again, we will have modeled a life skill that is worth more than any grade. In fact, many students responded that they appreciated hearing about how we acknowledge our own weaknesses, our own fallibility as people.

At any given time, for instance, I admit my own challenges with spelling. "Everything is a rough draft," I admit. "Inevitably, I find mistakes. But spellcheck is my friend and I use the resources that exist to help people like me who don't have a knack for it."

I've "fessed up" to all sorts of things. It's amazing what comes up in a classroom when you think it might help students learn something. I've confessed that I have terrible penmanship, which is why I type on the whiteboard instead of write on it. I've admitted that I was not a great, stellar student, and it took me forever (we're talking years after graduating from college) to figure out what I wanted be. I have a tendency to procrastinate, and blew opportunities when doors were open to me. I've shown kids two different color socks from getting dressed in the morning in a dark room. I've talked about being geographically dyslexic with no inner compass to guide my way from school to home. It's crazy the confessions you make when you are freed from pretending you have to know it all.

Of course, admitting my own struggles, and not being shut down by them, comes with reflection. And for many students, this kind of reflection is fairly new and bruises them with each realization.

Starting them on that journey takes targeted questions. In a specific student survey on growth mindset, I asked some of my struggling students, my LTELLs – the Long-Term English Language Learners – about what went through their heads when they faced assessments or more rigorous activities. These are the students who have been in this country for at least 7 years yet continue to show little to no literacy growth. Typically, these students show a dropout rate of over 25%. It is telling to see some of their responses:

> *"I shut down when there is a whole page of reading and no color."*
>
> *"I have negative thoughts like I feel like I can't do good."*
>
> *"When I see huge questions that come with reading I give up."*
>
> *"I'm not interested in it. When I'm interested in something . . . I would want to do it and do better."*
>
> *"When I would run out of thoughts, I always type or write something different to fill in the space."*

And it doesn't even occur to them that these thoughts are within their control. The great sadness is that each of these quotes represent students who give up in the face of failure. Many of our lessons, therefore, focus on how to move around, climb over, and plow through these habitual thoughts before the student academically collapses.

Out of curiosity, I also asked my honors students, the same age group as my LTELLs, what a growth mindset was. Their initial responses proved they logically knew the definition. Here are just a few:

> *"Someone with a growth mindset accepts failure and works to get better. Someone with a fixed mindset does nothing about it and stays the same."*

> *"When you have a growth mindset, you are willing to learn, expanding your academic achievements. You make mistakes, and you learn from them."*

> *"A mindset automatically sets an academic tone in your mind. If you want to succeed, you set in your mind to make big strides (or vice versa)."*

Nevertheless, despite the fact that they talked a great game, these students don't always necessarily walk the walk, as it were. After all, many of these kinds of high-level kids rarely take huge risks for fear of failure, and when failure does occur, you'd think the student's life had come to an end. Sure, they knew what growth mindset was, but when failure happened, they often still allowed it to collapse their spirit.

The key to help all students accept failure as a necessity in their own growth is to take our own risks and become transparent when they fail.

> "The key to help all students accept failure as a necessity in their own growth, is to model failure ourselves."

The bottom line, however, isn't just about feeling comfortable with failure; it's about achieving more by reflecting on failure. A summary of research by Carol S. Dweck and Lisa Sorich Blackwell (n.d.) has shown that

> students with a growth mindset had an upward trajectory in mathematics grades over seventh and eighth grade, while those who viewed their intelligence as a fixed quality did not. This was true even though students had equal levels of prior achievement: students who believed that their intelligence was malleable did

better than did equally able students who viewed their intelligence as an unchangeable, fixed "entity."

So, it's vital that students see our humanity as people who fail and get back up to try again. It's the power of *yet*.

Carol Dweck (2014) also spoke about this topic in her TEDTalk "The Power of Believing You Can Improve," when she acknowledged the "power of yet." The word *yet* grants people the understanding "that you are on a learning curve. It gives you a path into the future."

"It's the power of *yet*."

The role of teaching has evolved. No longer are we the carriers of knowledge, giving it to students and assessing if they can repeat facts successfully. We are, instead, tasked with teaching students how to find answers themselves. And it all starts with a simple three-word phrase: "I don't know."

Adopting a comfortable "I don't know" attitude is far more accurate for what we need to do as educators now rather than pretending we know it all. It sounds counterintuitive, I know. But in school, where every client is a work in progress, we need to cultivate a certain excitement in not knowing something. Modeling an excited "I don't know" attitude is the brass doorknob that opens the portal to finding answers together.

At the start of each year, I have to train students that I will not be feeding them answers, and students will not be copying my notes from the board. I will not hand out copies of words and definitions for them to study or give them fill-in-the-blank close paragraphs that we will all fill in together.

Rather, I will teach them how to develop questions.

And when they ask me for answers, I will happily and without embarrassment, reply with, "I don't know."

I will also teach them that when I ask them a question it's OK if they say, "I don't know." I won't make them feel bad for not knowing the answer. Instead, I will spend vital time teaching them that when "I don't know" pops into one's head, it is the trigger to find out.

For me, the guide in the room, that means making sure that my own attitude does not reflect our society's assumption that "I don't know" is a weakness.

"I don't know" has been so negatively ingrained that just the mere inkling of it tickling a student's brain can shut down learning. But to make "I don't know" a more positive phrase takes targeted lessons in empowering students to conquer their own confusion. It's important to permit them confusion, to permit them to admit that the pathway before them is blocked with overgrown foliage and weeds. Then you hand them a mental machete to clear the way themselves.

To do that takes a teacher who enjoys modeling his or her own confusion and isn't threatened by not knowing. Educator and author Sheridan Blau once said, "Honor confusion." The phrase "I don't know" is one that both honors confusion and stimulates the process of clearing it up (Wolpert-Gawron, 2014).

WHAT BEING MORE HUMAN LOOKS LIKE IN THE CLASSROOM

There are many strategies to humanize yourself and your classroom that also integrate your content area.

1. **Stray from the textbook**. Bring in examples of your content area from places outside the traditional textbook. Show you're thinking of the material and of their enthusiasm of it by bringing in something you found on your own time. Maybe even create a display where kids can show their own enthusiasm by bringing in examples of the content themselves.

2. **Create a Classroom Constitution with your input as well**. Create a contract at the start of the school year that not only incorporates their promises about behaving professionally both online and offline, but adds your own contributions as well. You are also a member of the community after all.

3. **Create a way for students to give you feedback**. Use a Google Form or other survey tool at the ends of the units that prove you really want to hear their opinions of the material and how it was delivered/learned. That kind of respect for their feedback goes a long way in helping them own the content themselves.

4. **Think about the issues a student brings into the classroom that might be shared in an unspoken way**. What are their nonverbal cues that something is amiss? Read the student and know that being a Work in Progress sometimes means not being able to communicate their needs. Approach a student and try to help them translate their own cues.

5. **Honor their workload.** Be respectful of how much work our students have per day/week/quarter/whatever. If it's not necessary, don't assign it. If you can give an extension, give it. If you can have students set their own deadlines, do it. If you can present upcoming assignments in different ways to honor the variety of learners in the classroom, do that too. In other words, have a weekly agenda, but also give them an overview of a quarter or semester so students can plan accordingly. My high school teacher Mrs. Dunn always said (in her southern drawl if you want to really hear this in your head): "Any teacher who thinks they have a greater workload than a dedicated student is crazy. Y'all have more work per day than I ever could." Depending on the teacher, this might be debatable, but the idea is valid.

6. **Find ways for students to share their interests**. Just as students who know more about you will be more engaged in your class, you will be more engaged with them if you've found ways to learn about them beyond the scope of academic learning. Start a public calendar with events on it that students can add that share their concerts, games, and other events. Create assignments that ask them to mine their own lives for examples. Ask them about themselves and make sure you follow up throughout the school year on that interest. Make sure it isn't just a one-hit assignment, but a conversation starter that can be ongoing. You might find someone bringing in an example of an arch from local architecture, but you also might see an example of a trajectory from a football toss.

7. **Give students strategies to manage their own feelings.** Leaving students to their own devices in terms of managing their emotions doesn't make them stronger; it abandons them. Conversely, if we can teach our students the tools to manage feelings that corrupt their achievement academically, behaviorally, and character-wise, they will

feel more cared for. And it doesn't take much. This can involve giving students the vocabulary to describe more angry feelings or providing them the time to journal about them or talk them out. It can be about giving them breathing strategies to help calm destructive feelings or about sharing your own moments of feeling down. Create an environment in which you, the teacher, acknowledge that students have negative feelings that can affect their achievement. Students will feel you care for them when you give a nod to the many emotions stirring within them at this time in their life.

8. **Celebrate uniqueness and passion as an ongoing theme in your classroom.** For instance, you can analyze Apple's "Think Different" ads through a persuasive lens or bring in biographies of people who thought a little off-center and brought change to the world.

9. **Have students participate in gathering real-world examples of mistakes.** Have them take pictures of inaccurate facts on billboards or misused words out there in the world beyond school. For instance, Weird Al Yankovic once shot a 15-sec video on his phone from what looked to be a Trader Joe's. In it, he pans up to a sign that reads, "15 Items or Less." He tapes the word *fewer* over the word *less,* turns the camera on himself, and rolls his eyes. That's all it takes for a lesson to be learned. The link to the video is on the companion website: http://resources .corwin.com/justaskus.

10. **Have students find evidence of failures in the lives of those they admire.** Check out videos and other records that have curated such stories. Another video, *Famous Failures* is available on the companion website.

11. **Share stories of yourself and your family as examples**. When talking about velocity, share when your father won a lottery to drive a racecar for a charity event. When naming characters in a narrative, tell them why you named your own kids what you did. When teaching measurement, tell about that time your husband just couldn't level the shelf correctly and had to do it three times before the picture wouldn't slide off the wood. It helps when the kids can picture you as a human, and not just as a teacher.

12. **Think aloud**. This one simple strategy is at the heart of everything. Think aloud. Narrate what you do and why you do things. Keep talking. Let them in. What are you connecting to and how? While you're reading that paragraph from the science textbook on the stars, share that the B-story in your head while you're reading is the night sky you saw over the summer at a national park. Let the kids into your thinking process, and you will have shared your personality and your expertise with them.

13. **Model how to use search engines to answer questions about which you don't know the answer.** Be very transparent and public with how and when you use a search browser. Model how to use Internet searches efficiently and safely so that "I don't know" can really mean, "Wait! Let me find out!" Teach them how to use the Google Advanced Search page, how to read a Wikipedia article with a critical eye, and how to identify a questionable website. Students should be able to be comfortable with not knowing an answer, but must then be shown repeatedly how to use the tools that exist to find the answers themselves.

I want to end this chapter on the following: School is not like that Las Vegas ad. What happens in your classroom *doesn't* stay in your classroom. What happens in your room ripples out beyond your notice. As Kimberly, a middle schooler, states

"I like when my teachers make the lesson fun. . . . It helps me focus more while walking out of the classroom happy and ready to go to my next class."

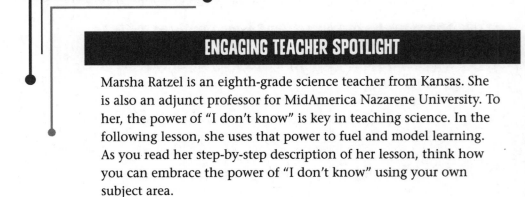

ENGAGING TEACHER SPOTLIGHT

Marsha Ratzel is an eighth-grade science teacher from Kansas. She is also an adjunct professor for MidAmerica Nazarene University. To her, the power of "I don't know" is key in teaching science. In the following lesson, she uses that power to fuel and model learning. As you read her step-by-step description of her lesson, think how you can embrace the power of "I don't know" using your own subject area.

OVERVIEW

Science is all about asking and answering questions about how the world works. Once you accept that premise, you realize that there will be many questions to which you don't know the answer. That's a good thing. This matches the spirit of a middle schooler to always be challenging and asking *why* and *how come*. Instead of labeling it as rebellion, we frame it as curiosity and finding one's ability to answer his or her own questions.

When a student asks me one of those questions, I quickly say, "I don't know, but *we* can find out." The beginning of the year is always when we talk about a couple of things that are relevant to that answer. First, the rate at which knowledge is changing is exponential. No one knows the answers to all questions, so being a good researcher of answers is key. The key to a lifetime of not knowing, is going and finding. I try to impart an attitude of adventure and discovery. . . . Students don't quite know how to react when you are learning side-by-side with them. . . . There is something so innocent about my "grown-up" eighth graders and I exploring the unknown together. It gives us a little cement for teacher/student relationship building.

STEP-BY-STEP

Learning how energy turned into matter at the start of the universe is a big idea. No one really knows the "right" answer, and it's a perfect place to emphasize that science doesn't "prove" anything . . . because by the time my eighth graders are my age, the cutting-edge science may have very well changed.

Since I don't feel capable of leading this discussion, I bought a copy of the series *How the Universe Works,* and we watch the Big Bang episode in eight chunks.

Here's how this works:

1. We start off writing the big question "How does the universe work?" on an empty page in their science spirals. They give answering the question a shot before we even start . . . good way to know how much they've learned in the end.

2. I built a viewing guide for them . . . each last three parts have several agree/disagree statements students read and

mark before we watch. While they are watching, they are trying to find evidence to support or refute their checkmark. Of course, students are encouraged to change their mind as new evidence is given. (Hint, hint)

3. Then we discuss. Sometimes it's facts they've seen.

4. After our discussion, students try to summarize what they're thinking into one- to three-sentence summaries.

5. At the midpoint, I have them return to their Aha! page where the big question sits, and they are asked to write a new answer to the big question.

6. And then they must use their arts and crafts supplies to create something that represents that understanding, a creation that fits in a 3" x 5" box that conveys the concept/feeling. It is in this creating process where we have huge discussions about what clouds of gas and dust must look like.

7. Everyone shares and gallery walks . . . and we're off to another chunk. We do lots of woo-ahhhh's. And students are free to change, update, and revise their creation if they see something that is inspirational. (If you can't tell, we learn from the movie, from my background research, the textbook and *each other*. I'm building a team.)

8. At the end, we talk about how the explosion of this infinitely small, infinitely hot spec of energy exploded and started matter. Or at least, that is our best understanding at this point. Students walk away having wrestled some of the biggest questions in theoretical physics, having realized that energy can turn (in very special circumstances) into matter, matter can turn into energy and that science really never has a definitive answer . . . only what the evidence shows.

9. On the last day, students write and share their final Aha! that attempts to answer, "How does the universe work?" My goal for this sharing is mostly for them to see how sophisticated their answers have become and how much they've learned. Plus, since it's early in the year, they get comfortable sharing and leading in front of the class. They are usually quite shocked and pleased at how far their learning has come, and it gives me a chance to tell them how accomplished I see them becoming during the year (in an honest way).

10. This lesson sets the stage for thinking about energy and we launch into model building atoms to learn about the structure and properties of matter.

REFLECTION

This lesson takes about a week of arguing, getting stumped, realizing you are in good company and still being willing to wonder and question. It's also a great place to start a yearlong sifting/sorting process by asking, Is this something that is knowable, or is it beyond the eighth grader's ability to know at this time? Lots of things we find out are actually questions that nuclear chemists are working on in their labs right now.

I especially love the conversations where "we" go and find out . . . and then talk about what our discoveries mean. Students bring what they find on the Internet, what their dad said, what their mom said, and even what books said. Then collectively we sort through the dump truck of new information and try to formulate a conclusion.

Finally, not knowing the answers to all student questions is a great thing. It's exciting and takes a teacher and the class conversation to unexpected places of adventure and inquiry. Plus, it's a simple way to bond.

DISCUSSION QUESTIONS

1. Based on your content area, what are three stories from your own life that can align to three standards you are trying to convey to the students?

2. What are two examples in your own life in which you failed miserably? What strategies did you use to move forward from your failure? How long did it take you to rebound from the failure or criticism?

3. How old were you when you began to internalize the need to move forward from disappointment?

4. Think of your favorite, albeit more traditionally crafted, lesson. How might you modify this beloved lesson to include your own experiences as supplemental material?

Photo courtesy of Davis Lester

CHAPTER SEVEN

HELP US CREATE SOMETHING WITH WHAT WE'VE LEARNED

"I want to actually have experience doing whatever it is that I am learning."

OVERVIEW

To this day, I remember the project I created in eighth-grade English after reading Shakespeare's *Twelfth Night*. Ms. Suave had us create an LP (I know, I just dated myself. An LP is a record album for those who don't know). Anyway, she had us create an album of "songs" that reflected the themes and characters of the play. What we all created was album art and a list of poetry in the liner notes that included iambic pentameter as well as loose rhyme schemes peppered with humor from the Bard's work. I remember well that my favorite song I wrote was "I'd Rather Eat an Anchovy Than to Marry You," an attempt at a humorous ballad in the voice of Olivia and set to the timely tune of Bonnie Tyler's "Total Eclipse of the Heart."

I remember it all vividly, and it was because my teacher found a way for us to create something with what we'd learned that went beyond a literary analysis or simple book report.

Given the impact creating had on my own learning, it came as no surprise that hands-on learning and, by extension, creating something with what they've learned, also ranked a spot on the student engagement survey. While one can tease them apart, many students mentioned them both as if indicating that they understood that interacting with material in a hands-on way was a part of the process used in creation. The survey indicates that students are most engaged when they create, but it also resides as the top tier of developmental categories, according to the most recent Bloom's Taxonomy pyramid, shown in Figure 7.1. It is the level that supersedes all others.

"Making the stuff or doing something instead of just sitting and listening is what makes me excited about a class."

—Tara R., Tenth Grade

CONSUMPTION VERSUS CREATION

In fact, the Center for Accelerated Learning (n.d.) says, "Learning is creation, not consumption. Knowledge is not something a learner absorbs, but something a learner creates." This issue of consumption versus creation is a tricky one for our educational system because our system is set up beautifully to support the former when in fact we need to embrace the latter.

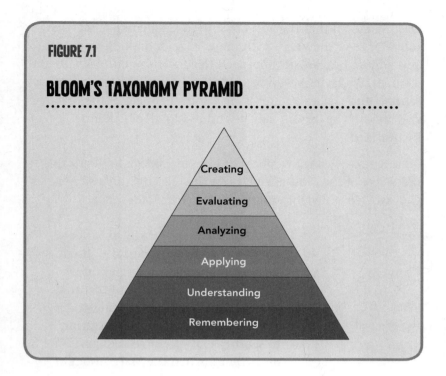

FIGURE 7.1

BLOOM'S TAXONOMY PYRAMID

Creating

Evaluating

Analyzing

Applying

Understanding

Remembering

Not only does adopting a more creative-centric implementation mean a more effective educational model, but it means a more engaging one as well.

The current educational model is going through a rapid metamorphosis of sorts. True, our adoption of Bloom's pushes us in the right direction, but the technological tools and devices of today also help to move us from that consumption model of yore to a more creation-oriented model. Nevertheless, inertia runs deep; and many schools and classrooms still struggle to shift their practice from the "sage on the stage" model. It's hard to move an entire system, particularly one that was once steeped in trickle-down implementation strategies.

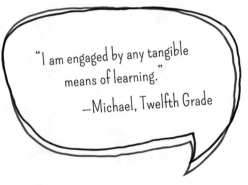

"I am engaged by any tangible means of learning."

—Michael, Twelfth Grade

"Learning is creation, not consumption. Knowledge is not something a learner absorbs, but something a learner creates."

—Center for Accelerated Learning

What I mean by this is that our educational system was once totally modeled after what supposedly worked for adults. Face-forward, group lesson lectures were echoed in the halls of our colleges and universities, and our high schools, middle, and elementary schools mimicked those, following suit. Now, some would argue that this model doesn't work for everyone, but it was the model that the adult attention span could somewhat tolerate. Over the years, with knowledge of brain development and a more humanistic approach to education, our primary and elementary classes began to shift. Nevertheless, many secondary schools and classes still felt (and continue to echo) the practices still seen in the lecture halls found in higher-education institutions.

Research has begun to argue that even for college students, this model is not the most effective one. In a recent University of Chicago–led study, for example, researchers found that

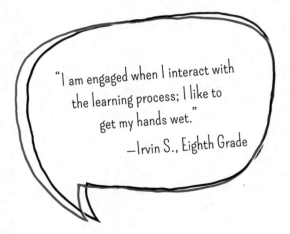

"I love hands on projects in class, I remember the things I have done during the projects much better than the things I have taken notes on."

—Elise M.

"I am engaged when I interact with the learning process; I like to get my hands wet."

—Irvin S., Eighth Grade

[s]tudents who physically experience scientific concepts understand them more deeply and score better on science tests. . . . Brain scans showed that students who took a hands-on approach to learning had activation in sensory and motor-related parts of the brain when they later thought about concepts such as angular momentum and torque. Activation of these brain areas was associated with better quiz performance by college physics students who participated in the research. (Ingmire, 2015)

Despite the research, higher education is shifting at its own pace, and the K–12 system can't wait for it to make a more dramatic shift in its practice in order to signal their own. Even the secondary levels need to begin morphing our own practice to a hands-on, purposeful, and creation-based model now. This isn't just because it's more engaging or even because hands-on learning shows greater results on test scores. It's also because our world has changed and requires students to emerge from our schools ready to think, create, and own their learning.

The *Huffington Post* reports that

[f]or generations, engineering education has been a *consumption* process. The role of the student is to sit, observe, and absorb while the instructor "pours" knowledge into eager minds. Such an approach may have served us well in the past, but in today's global and technological world, we need to change the emphasis of education to that of a *creation* process—one in which students take charge of and play an active role in their education. . . . In other words, we need to help students move from being consumers to creators of their educations . . . . It's about rethinking the concept of ownership in education and implementing a support system that enables and allows students to claim control of the learning process. (Somerville & Goldberg, 2012)

"For me, I like and learn hands-on. When teachers tell me something, it comes through, but not as much as if I and peers did it hands-on. If I am reading something, it also does come through, but, again, hands-on is best for me. Like in science, instead of being told a concept, we would do experiments proving it."

—Gemma L., Middle Schooler

Additionally, a 2009 study at Purdue University found that eighth graders—many of whom were English Language Learners—succeeded at a higher rate in showing comprehension of engineering concepts when encouraged to learn those concepts through hands on learning rather than traditional textbook and lecture-based methods.

Melissa Dark (2009), the assistant dean for strategic planning in the College of Technology at Purdue reports that

[i]n every area we tested, the students who were involved in a hands-on project learned more and demonstrated a deeper understanding of the issues than the traditional group. . . . This is a significant finding because it proves that with some students—especially groups traditionally

"What really engages me is hands on lessons like in science when we get to make our own batteries or in technology where we use cool sites like scratch. Those lessons that really engage me always let me be a part of it let me do the work not just have it already set up and all we have to do is press the go button."

—Dylan, Sixth Grade

underrepresented in science and engineering—the book-and-lecture format may not be the best way to engage students in learning.

The eighth graders were being tasked to study human impacts on water and water quality. Half of the group was taught through textbook reading, lectures, and tests, followed by a small culminating project. The other half were tasked to build a water purification device, and less than 10% of this focus group's classroom time utilized lecture-based, whole-group teaching.

According to Dark (2009),

The results showed that the students who built the purification device had higher scores and a much higher degree of improvement than the traditionally taught students on both true/false and open-ended questions, [and] that while all students in the design group made gains, they were especially significant with students whose native language isn't English.

"What really engages me when it comes to learning, is being hands on. In my anatomy class, we do a couple labs a week to demonstrate the topic we are learning. This is one of my favorite classes because it's not just lecture, lecture and more lecture."

—Brandan S., Twelfth Grade

Hands-on learning, the research proves, makes the learning more concrete and "sticky" for those engineering students. In fact, it seems that the sciences understood the value of hands-on learning early on. After all, with labs and the scientific process, "learning by doing" seems to go hand in hand with their standards. However, these methods cannot be used during traditional science labs alone. All classrooms should be adopting these same theories of interacting with the material.

ENGAGE WITH THE CONTENT!

This video shows some of the products in my own classroom, which students have created as artifacts of their knowledge. Also, check out the interview with teacher Susie Aames and some of my own students as they discuss the power of creating over mere consumption. As you watch the video, think of the following:

- What are the different modalities that can be tapped into when you allow students to create something with your content?

- How comfortable do you feel with giving students choice in what they create to prove their learning?

- How does creation relate to student independent learning?

Video 7.1 Let Them Create

CREATING AND MAKING IN EVERY SUBJECT AREA

It's interesting to note that while much of the research out there in a consumption educational model versus a creation educational model seems to focus on STEM, we clearly can't segregate an engagement strategy to engineering and math alone. Every subject matter should adopt creation over consumption; it just requires a different way of looking how we reframe our relationship with learning.

I've seen this in a symbolic way as I've explored 3D printing. It's been amazing to see the level of engagement from students when seeing an object from their brain appear on the heated bed of the machine before them. The machine brought to life the item that, prior to that moment, had only lived within the imagination of a middle school student. Creation made concrete.

> "What engages me as a student is interesting, different, projects. Projects like making a religion or buzzfeeds lists. Also projects like making a mathematic park or a brochure for ancient Greece have you learn and inspires me to be creative."
>
> —Holly L.

The recent increase in makerspaces seems to reflect an understanding of how vital hands-on learning can be. Makerspaces support the design thinking process, the method of brainstorming and visualizing, prototyping, and finalizing that mimics classic engineering strategies.

"Hands on learning, the research proves, makes the learning more concrete and 'sticky.'"

FIGURE 7.2

THE DESIGN PROCESS

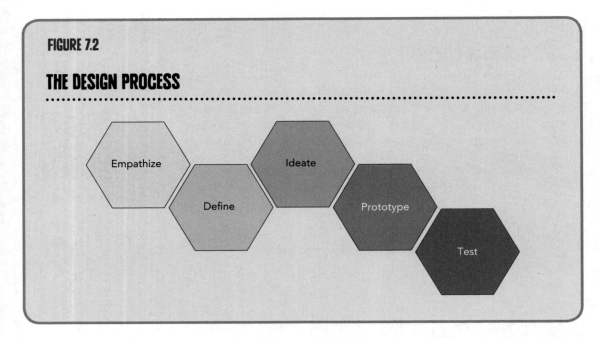

However, you don't need a 3D printer, or even a makerspace, to have your students actualize their thoughts or participate in design thinking. All you need are strategies that help students bring their learning to life.

In fact, I would argue that design thinking and a makerspace mentality have a role to play in every classroom and, in fact, provides a structure that any subject area can use metaphorically to encourage more hands-on and creation-based learning.

For instance, think about the writing process. Typically, it goes like this:

Brainstorming/Developing the prompt

Drafting/Peer review

Revising/Editing

Finalizing/Publication

But if we think of writing *as* making, then we have the opportunity to trigger a more hands-on method of teaching writing.

Brainstorming	IS	Defining and ideating
Drafting	IS	Prototyping/crowdsourcing feedback
Revising	IS	Tweaking those prototypes based on feedback
Finalizing/ Publication	IS	Testing

It's in this stage of finalizing that one can really embrace the creation concept. After all, websites use writing. Commercials require scripting. Promotional campaigns need to be persuasive. There are endless ways to create in the writing class.

I would also argue that design thinking and the makerspace mentality also have a role to play in the math classroom or history classroom, our electives, and our PE classes.

In PE, for instance, students can create digital how-to manuals using iBooks or Google Slideshows that show annotated photos of students using the proper form when playing a sport, step-by-step rules in how to play a game, and history of specific activities.

In history, students can create "What if" slideshows that analyze what would happen if some event had been deleted from our timeline. These slideshows can show the ripple through time of what events would look like had this moment in time not occurred.

Look, we know the old adage.

People generally remember

10% of what they READ,

20% of what they HEAR,

30% of what they SEE,

50% of what they HEAR and SEE,

70% of what they SAY, and

90% of what they SAY as they DO a thing.

So allow students to learn through doing in any subject area. Allow them to create with what they've learned, and interact with their content in a more hands-on way.

"The one thing I as a student DO NO like is sitting in a classroom listening to a lecture or filling out a worksheet. I think I learn more and discover more thing on my own with these hands-on experiences opposed to sitting at a desk and doing a test."

—Halle F., Seventh Grade

"One of the ways which I am drawn into lessons would be creating visuals. For example, in my Science class, we just started learning about National Parks. . . . A month later, we found ourselves in groups constructing floats. We were so committed to them, and everybody, for once, was excited to enter the classroom. . . . While making the floats, we had learned so much about our parks, everyone in the class shined. Creating models of what we are learning about is fun and exciting."

—Bridget P., Middle Schooler

CREATION AND THE ROLE OF TECHNOLOGY

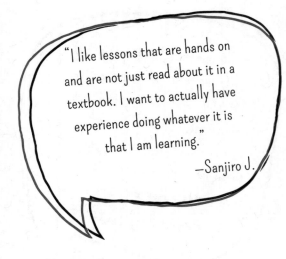

"I like lessons that are hands on and are not just read about it in a textbook. I want to actually have experience doing whatever it is that I am learning."

—Sanjiro J.

The accessibility of educational technology has actually made creation much more accessible to the average learner. From iPads to Chromebooks, there are more students connected to the Internet and utilizing technology than ever before. According to a 2015 report, more than three-fourths of our schools are meeting the FCC Internet access goals (Camera, 2015), and more and more schools have adopted some kind of device for their students. And these numbers are only growing.

In fact, when we look at the Godfather of all content creators, YouTube, we'll see that over 300 hours of content is created and uploaded every minute! ("36 Mind-Blowing YouTube Facts," 2017). From there, it's only natural that once students are exposed to all of the creation going on out there, they would want to participate in that as well. And the proof is out there that they already are.

Author, educator, and speaker Clay Shirkey (2010) recognized in his TEDTalk "How Cognitive Surplus Will Change the World" that people want to create, that technology has opened a floodgate of creation, and it's up to us to help funnel that desire into quality artifacts that not only create, but have an impact on our world.

"Consistent fun projects that allow creativity as a form for education. Science would have exciting experiments, famous historical scenes acted out in plays in front of the class. . . . And because I love creativity and learning, we can make a way to make school a hybrid of both!"

—Antonio C.

In his speech, he nails the fact that the 20th century focused on helping people consume, but that with the onset of the Internet and devices, our goals must shift, and he identifies the evidence that proves our students want that shift as well.

> [W]hat we're seeing is that people weren't couch potatoes because we liked to be. We were couch potatoes because that was the only opportunity given to us. We still like to consume,

of course. But it turns out we also like to create, and we like to share. And it's those two things together—ancient human motivation and the modern tools to allow that motivation to be joined up in large-scale efforts—that are the new design resource. And using cognitive surplus, we're starting to see truly incredible experiments in scientific, literary, artistic, political efforts. Designing. . . . We're also getting, of course, a lot of LOLcats. LOLcats are cute pictures of cats made cuter with the addition of cute captions. . . . LOLcats are the stupidest possible creative act. . . . But here's the thing: The stupidest possible creative act is still a creative act. Someone who has done something like this, however mediocre and throwaway, has tried something, has put something forward in public. And once they've done it, they can do it again, and they could work on getting it better. (Shirkey, 2010)

So it's up to educators to help students not only recognize quality results of creative endeavors; it's up to us to help them create quality themselves.

WHAT CREATION LOOKS LIKE IN THE CLASSROOM

There are many tools out there that can help students create so that they are not only contributing to our society, but they are engaged as well. This marriage of creation and contribution gives purpose to the learning, which, in turn, interests students in any subject area.

Students can, for instance, do any of the following:

"This that might engage me as a student, would be, 'hands on' assessments, where experiments and building would be involved. It would might encourage students to come to school, knowing that they are both learning and having fun. For example, in math, when you are learning about capacity (ie. volume, area, etc.) you could use, legos for example. Legos are both something that you can learn from, and children's toys. They can piece together cubes for geometry, and build shapes to find the area, and volume of !! It's a win—win situation, the teacher get their students to be engaging in their work, and the students are learning and are having fun at the same time !!"

—Christy C.

1. **Develop a promotional campaign.** Have students develop a website using Weebly to promote a solution to a problem. They can also use Picstich to create a collage of images to create an argument and send a message on that issue. They can create an infographic of data, text, and symbols using Piktochart to prove their findings.

2. **Create a public service announcement.** Use persuasive writing and digital storytelling programs like iMovie to create a commercial that pitches a point of view. Use Powtoons to create an animated speech or dialogue about a topic that looks amazingly like those used in RSAnimate.

3. **Build a lesson to teach others about a topic.** That's right; building a lesson itself is also creation. Teach students how to create a hyperdoc using Padlet or even a Google Doc or Thinglink. Combine them with a Google Form using questions developed by the students themselves and have them administer the informal assessment to peers after teaching the lesson to other students. Have students develop screencasts of skills or mini-lessons using programs like EduCreation or Screencastify for Chrome.

4. **Present a speech.** Guide students in the formats of a TEDTalk or Ignite speech. Details are as follows:

   TEDTalk format: memoir anecdote + background information + argument + evidence + call to action

   Ignite speech: 20 slides only, 15 seconds each that are automatically advanced, 5 minutes total, very image-based slides

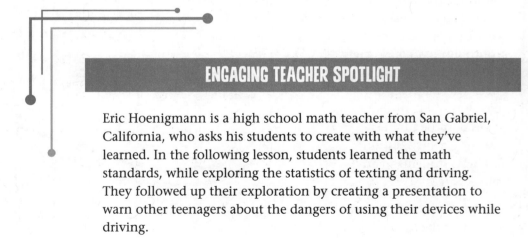

ENGAGING TEACHER SPOTLIGHT

Eric Hoenigmann is a high school math teacher from San Gabriel, California, who asks his students to create with what they've learned. In the following lesson, students learned the math standards, while exploring the statistics of texting and driving. They followed up their exploration by creating a presentation to warn other teenagers about the dangers of using their devices while driving.

TEXTING AND DRIVING: IT CAN WAIT!!!

By Eric Hoenigmann—A Math Conversion Lesson

Materials Needed: iPad or Computer, Cellphone, headphone (next to iPad cart), paper, and pencil.

Project Length: 3 Days

Day 1: Activity and research

Day 2: Work on project with table members

Day 3: Present slideshow to class

Take out your cell phone and look at the last text you sent. Would that text be worth dying for? Definitely not. Sending or looking at that text, tweet, post, or email from behind the wheel can be deadly. In fact, studies show those who text while driving are much more likely to be in crash.

Partner up with a classmate at your table and follow the activity directions below. Be mindful of the fact that a peer in the class may have experienced a car accident themselves or had a loved one be injured or killed by one. This can be a very sensitive issue for some so be careful with what you say.

Each student should do the tasks on their own sheet of paper.

First, you will work with a partner to do Tasks 1–6.

Second, work on Tasks 7–12 on your own.

Third, work with your whole table on Task 13.

1. Compose your own text response to the message, *"What are you doing later?"* Imagine that one hand is on the driving wheel and text with the free hand. Have your partner time how long it takes you to respond. Record your time and then switch roles.

2. Put your phone away. Use the discussion starter below to help think about the following question. *How far, in feet, would your car have traveled while going 30 mph (miles per hour)?*

(*Note:* The length of a football field is 360 feet.)

3. Think about being distracted for this length of time and distance. *What could happen if you were driving through a residential or commercial area?*

4. *How far, in feet, would your car have traveled while going 70 mph?*

5. Think about being distracted for this length of time and distance. *What could happen if you were driving on the freeway?*

6. *If you are comfortable, share any car accident experiences you or a loved one have had.*

7. Look at the following link for key statistics on this topic: www.distraction.gov/stats-research-laws/facts-and-statistics .html

CALIFORNIA LAW

Read www.wklaw.com/texting-while-driving-could-land-you-in-jail/

8. What is the law in California for texting and driving? Do you think they should be less or more strict and why?

9. Watch the following videos, *using headphones,* to develop a better understanding of the potential consequences of texting and driving. Only watch videos from the links provided. (*Warning:* Some of the videos are quite graphic and intense.)

RESOURCES FOR TASK 9

(*Note:* These videos are available on the book's companion website.)

- *Accident on a Freeway: Skip to 0:30*

- *Accident on a Highway*

- *An Accident in Slow Motion*

- *A Survivor's Story*

- *Convicted of Vehicular Manslaughter 1*

- *Convicted of Vehicular Manslaughter 2*

10. What are some of your thoughts after watching the videos?

11. Even if you think you are a "great" texter, it only takes a split second for you to forever alter or end your life or the life of someone else. If you haven't prior, hopefully you will now take the pledge to never use your phone and drive. Do you pledge to not use your phone and drive?

12. Being a passenger in a car with someone who is using their phone while driving can put you in just as much danger. You must have the courage to speak up as well. When a passenger, do you pledge to speak up and insist that the driver not use their phone and drive?

When you get behind the wheel remember this: "With great power comes great responsibility."

13. With all the members at your table, you will now work together to help convince friends and family of the dangers of using their phone and driving. Use the information acquired to create a Google slideshow that you will present. In addition to the slideshow, your table must create one of the following:

   - Radio public service announcement

   - Commercial film

   - Brochure

   - Poster to hang at high schools and colleges

   - Billboard advertisement

Choose any medium you like and ask your teacher for the materials you need. Use statistics, tables, charts, images, and/ or film clips to evoke a greater response from your audience. If you are comfortable, you can share a personal experience. Your grade will be determined by the content and quality of your presentation. The two main questions used when grading are "Was it convincing?" and "Was it professional?" Use the tips below for presenting. You will receive a *zero* if you treat the topic as something funny. If using humor, do so in a tasteful manner.

TEACHER REFLECTION

The texting and driving project was a great success with my high school students. Students took the project very seriously because it's based on a topic they can all relate to. The presentations were engaging and thought provoking.

DISCUSSION QUESTIONS

1. Thinking back on your own experience as a student. What was the most engaging artifact that you remember creating for any class?

2. How might a student use the Design Thinking process to help verify a math equation or analyze an event in history?

3. Think about a formal or informal assessment already tied to the end of a current lesson or unit. What can your students create that can prove their content knowledge?

4. Think of your favorite, albeit more traditionally crafted, lesson. How might you modify this beloved lesson to include creating something more hands on?

Photo courtesy of Davis Lester

CHAPTER EIGHT

TEACH US SOMETHING NEW IN A NEW WAY

"Open our eyes to something new."

OVERVIEW

When I first conducted the student engagement survey, no other response surprised me more than the recognition by multiple students that when they learn something new, they are most engaged. I mean, it seemed certainly obvious that learning new things was more exciting than hearing the same things over and over, year to year, but it wasn't until I got deeper into the research that I realized just how much time per school year was spent *not* learning new things.

THE DETRIMENTAL PRACTICE OF OVERREVIEWING

The reason, of course, for so much review over the course of a school year is because of testing. Federal tests, state tests, district tests, classroom tests, review for tests, it all equates to a tremendous amount of time spent on older material. It all equates to less time spent on the "Cool!" and "Eureka!" and more time stuck in repeat.

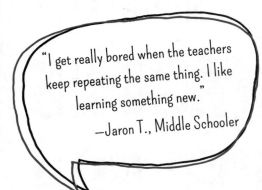

"I get really bored when the teachers keep repeating the same thing. I like learning something new."

—Jaron T., Middle Schooler

It's important to note that this isn't all the fault of what's dictated by the federal government. Of course, they might have some culpability here, but the burden of blame for overtesting and overreviewing falls on all educators' shoulders.

In a video message to *The Washington Post*, President Obama said that, in

moderation, smart, strategic tests can help us measure our kids' progress in school, and it can help them learn. . . . But I also hear from parents who, rightly, worry about too much testing, and from teachers who feel so much pressure to teach to a test that it takes the joy out of teaching and learning, both for them and for the students. (Strauss, 2015)

As a result, the president put a recommended limit on testing as 2.5% of instructional time in the classroom.

But the ripple effect was still tremendous, and it inevitably affects engagement.

The Washington Post later reported that

> it becomes clear that the time (and resources) dedicated to testing are actually much greater than the tests' duration. This is very important because when students are engaged in this testing process, they are not engaged in learning. And when teachers are engaged in this testing process, they are not engaged in teaching. (Strauss, 2015)

"I like when our teacher uses videos that show us the same topic but in different approaches on learning bird. This way I learn how different people think . . ."

—Rebecca L., Eleventh Grade

Despite the president's well-intentioned limitations, the merit of testing is still questionable as many of the students who fail are then stuck in the tar pit of drill-and-kill classes. These are classes that review and review and review with the assumption that reviewing material over and over will miraculously add up to fundamental knowledge acquisition. In fact, in the 2013 Education Nation Summit, experts stated that "[t]he test and punish model hasn't worked" (Long, 2013).

Additionally, Valerie Strauss reported, "There is no correlation between the amount of mandated testing time and the reading and math scores in grades four and eight on the National Assessment of Educational Progress (NAEP)" (Strauss, n.d.).

The English Language Learners and Special Ed students are constantly stuck in drill-and-kill models. If they don't prove via testing that they can move on from the fundamentals, then they are continuously stuck in the molasses of worksheets and review. This not only does nothing to engage them, but it stagnates their ability to think critically, a skill that has little to do with much of what they are drilled on. After all, a student might not understand how to describe a subject and predicate, but he or she still might be able to write a sentence based on an issue that is near and dear to their heart. Once that student produces that sentence, feedback can be given, and improvement can be made.

"What engages me as. Student is when we are learning something new and exciting and it makes me focus more on what we are learning because interesting topics always get my attention."

—Christopher N., Junior High

> "Something that engage my as a student is learning something new, not just stuff from textbooks but something related to the things that I am learning."
>
> —Qing Yuan

However, to lock that kid into drier methods of implementation does a disservice to what their brain is capable of learning.

Just look at an approximate breakdown of how much time is spent testing during a school year:

One week per year spent on federal and/or state mandated assessments.

One week per quarter spent on district testing.

One week per quarter to prep for the district assessment.

One quiz per week in many classrooms.

One test every 2 weeks in many classrooms.

The Washington Post further found that "[t]he heaviest testing load falls on the nation's eighth-graders, who spend an average of 25.3 hours during the school year taking standardized tests" (Strauss, 2015), while the Center for American Progress (n.d.) found that "52 percent of the assessments that students [in one local county] take are district mandated, while less than half are state required. In other words, over testing . . . might not be only a state and federal problem but a local problem as well."

> "I love to learn more about what is out there in our world, such as different kinds of math, and our history, and even different types of music. Not only that, but it is done in various, creative, new ways, like playing an educational game. It is often easier to get hooked onto something new, but also fun, meaning you are enjoying learning new things."
>
> —Jordan C., Seventh Grade

And once we get into test prep allocated time, the amount of instructional minutes drops dramatically. In a recent study by Central Washington University, *The Seattle Times* reported that over 18% of class time is devoted to test prep (Rowe, 2014).

When testing and prep is combined, we are talking over 20% of a student's instructional time spent in review. And this figure doesn't even account for the typical time spent during the school year reviewing the prior year's skills and content. In some districts and schools, that varies as widely as a full quarter up to a possible semester of review time before new content instruction even begins. Yawn.

Spiraling is another strategy, different from review. Spiraling is when, say, a concept is introduced in September and then returned to throughout the year, building on it each time. Spiraling is meant to combat the compartmentalized method of teaching that only allows a student to learn and succeed one time a year on a given concept.

Howard Johnston (2012), the author of *The Spiral Curriculum: Research into Practice*, wrote that there are three key elements to a successful spiral curriculum:

1. The student revisits a topic, theme or subject several times throughout their school career

2. The complexity of the topic or theme increases with each revisit

3. New learning has a relationship with old learning and is put in context with the old information

Notice that even when talking about a spiraling curriculum, it becomes vital that new information be presented and applied so that it isn't merely review.

So what can we do to combat this trend toward actively making our content stale? The good news is that there is much we can also do to take responsibility for the quality of both instruction and assessment so that both can feel much more fresh and, yes, even new.

First and foremost, we can adopt alternative forms of assessment and implementation. That is, we have to find new ways to present content to students. Even in a spiraling curriculum, we need to vary how we deliver the reviewed material so that, if anything, the content might be familiar, but the presentation would seem original.

"Sometimes the best way to get a students attention for something is to introduce it in a new light. A way that can relate to them. When I am learning about something that I have no passion for or I has no relation to what I do or care about then it's hard to take it seriously."

—Gisele S.

Repeating what we've done in the past, how we've done it, and then pressing repeat again, takes away from engaged learning and engaged teaching. And for the purposes of this book, and the goal of engaging students in the learning process, overtesting and overreviewing go against our goals.

ENGAGE WITH THE CONTENT!

Video 8.1 Teach Something New

This video highlights the importance of hitting new material and hitting review material using new methods. Hear from the students themselves as well as the teachers. As you watch their interviews, think about the following:

- Where do you find inspiration for new materials and methodologies?

- How much of your own content did students learn about in years prior?

- Is there any activity that you require from students that routinely bores you when it's time to grade their artifacts?

STEPPING OUT OF OUR WHEELHOUSE TO MODEL LEARNING

That's why it's important that we, as teachers, also keep seeking out what's new to us. A part of what we do needs to be less about content delivery and more about modeling how and why we learn. We need to be curating what's current in our content area and sharing with unabashed enthusiasm when something opens our eyes a little wider too.

> "What engages me as a student is getting to learn about new things. Learning about stuff I never knew before! And learning how to do things I never knew how to do! Also I love to work with people so we can compare answers and get help from them if i need it."
>
> —Brooklyn T. Portland, Middle Schooler

Triggering curiosity is no small feat. It takes modeling enthusiasm; and learning something new generates our own enthusiasm, even if it's something new about the content we've covered for years.

Think about it. Let's say you're clicking through your Twitter or Facebook feed and you stumble on a link in your content area. You realize it's a new factoid, a new perspective on an age-old topic. Maybe it's a new TEDTalk or graph with statistics, something that makes a concept more concrete. Maybe it's an infographic or photo, something that makes you furrow your brows and say, "Whaaa?!"

Speaking of this, I think one of the reasons why the whole world seems to be losing its mind over the Broadway production of *Hamilton* is because it presents a fresh take on a story we've all heard before. The power of learning something new is undeniable.

You have to bring that love of "Whaaa?!" into your own classroom. You have to model your own curiosity quotient. Our curiosity quotient is the hunger to learn that defines how we advance our knowledge of the world. According to the *Harvard Business Review,* a higher curiosity quotient can indicate more flexibility and help build a greater ability to handle complexity (Chamorro-Premuzic, 2014).

> "Repeating what we've done in the past, how we've done it, and then pressing repeat again, takes away from engaged learning and engaged teaching."

I can't think of a better example of learning through modeling than when I recently began fooling around with my school's 3D printer.

I didn't know what I was doing, but I figured that the interest in the tool itself, and my ignorance about how to use it, could help encourage students to learn the device with me. So a few students went through the tutorials with me, read the manual independently, and soon began printing originally designed gadgets, open source files, and little inventions almost to tease me about my far-slower learning curve. But that's what I love about adopting a new device to pilot in my classroom; I don't feel the need to be an expert in it; I feel the need to model my curiosity for it and the steps I might take to learn how to use it. In terms of 3D printing, the students soon pulled ahead in what I could tell them and became the experts themselves. As a result of seeing how I could leverage my own ignorance to model learning, I designed a class that used 3D printing to teach literacy and writing.

One of the things I actually really appreciate about the advent of the 3D printing in the classroom era is that it's one of the first technological tools that have appeared in our current students' lifetime, and as such, their discoveries have become a part of its evolution into a more mainstream tool. Additionally, it puts teachers and students on the same learning curve. We are learning

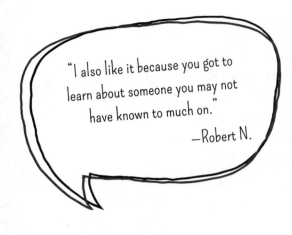

"I also like it because you got to learn about someone you may not have known to much on."

—Robert N.

hand-in-hand in this journey (Wolpert-Gawron, 2016).

Sure, it can lead to a big heapin' mess of vulnerability when you take on something totally out of your wheelhouse in front of the students. But it models how to question, how to stumble, and how to find joy in the journey of learning.

So think about your content area. What is a new take on a topic that you can bring to your classroom? What is a new device that you can bring in that you know nothing about? What new piece of information might help you trigger your own enthusiasm that can then, thereby, trigger your students' curiosity? How might you bring a new spin to your familiar curriculum?

WHAT OPENING EYES TO NEW CONCEPTS LOOKS LIKE IN THE CLASSROOM

But you don't have to dive into the latest tech tool du jour to present something new to your students.

It can be a different perspective in your current content.

It can be a new resource that takes your content deeper.

It can be from the voice of someone other than the classroom teacher.

It can be a new way to present the information.

It can be a new way to accept the outcome of their knowledge.

It can even be a process of allowing the students to learn their content independently so that they bring their own interpretation to the content.

Here are some activities and strategies to help bring newness into your classroom:

1. **Have the students explore a new tool or resource.** One of the ways I bring newness into my classroom is in sharing the resources I learn at various conferences and

webinars. However, I don't sift through the myriad of tools I learn about; instead, I assign them to small groups of students who then present their findings in a "blast" in front of the class. Here is the sequence of what I do when I develop a list of tools or resources that I want to explore:

a. I provide the list of app/materials/website/ programs/etc. to the students.

b. Students are broken up into small groups.

c. The groups select three to five resources to learn about.

d. The groups create a collaborative Google Slideshow. Each slide focuses on one of the resources.

e. Each slide includes the following: an image, a statement of purpose, how it can be used in the classroom, opinion of the product after exploration.

f. These tools are then added to my resource library on my classroom website so that students can access them for various projects and information.

2. **Bring an expert into the classroom.** This suggestion is also a huge part of project-based learning, but it really aligns with simply bringing a fresh voice into the classroom. When experts are brought in to lend their perspective to the students' learning, it always brings in something new for those students to think about.

3. **Confer with lower grades about their process and material.** It's always good to vertically articulate with the grades lower than your own. Don't wait for your school or district to

"What engages me is that how much they take the time to set up and teach us new things. We sit there and watch as the teacher talks us into a new world. For example in History class. We sit there knowing we are going to learn something new . . . apart from the book. She adds more and more onto it to and gives us more detail."

—Leah M.

"The thing that makes me wanna learn is using technology, peer work, and opening our eyes to something new."

—David Q.

> "As a student, the subject Science really engages me. I enjoy this subject because the knowledge is endless, meaning there are always new things to learn in the world of Science. Also, there are so many fields of Science to learn about and discover new things."
>
> —Margot H.

arrange for formal meetings; talk to people yourself. How often did a previous teacher hit this particular standard? Did the previous teacher already teach the biography of a specific author? Have students already participated in this experiment before? While there is, of course, the argument to go deeper with each repetition, have your students already dissected owl pellets for the past 2 years? Have your students already read *The Jacket* in subsequent language arts classes? Unless you plan on going deeper, presenting the information in a new way, or bringing in a fresh outlook on that particular lesson, you need to be aware that it might be review for many of your students.

4. **Follow people, subscribe to feeds, and become a current curator**. Continue to find newness in your professional development and learning. The more you have your finger on the pulse of current ideology, current discoveries, and current resources, the fresher your content will be in the classroom. For instance, while I've been teaching the monologue "All the World's a Stage" for years, I was really excited to find a recent commercial for upcoming BBC dramas that featured Benedict Cumberbatch saying the monologue to a montage of clips that helped to visualize the piece. You should have heard the class freak out when his face appeared on the screen! From Twitter to Facebook, iTunes U classes to pop culture feeds, keep feeding your own knowledge of your content area.

> "I personally think that my History teacher taught me a lot this year. I learn a new thing almost every single day, from politics, or even about music! I really like her class because I get to stress about work, then have a time to relax before working hard again. It is kind of like the ocean waves. My teacher pushes us to work extremely hard before letting us go."
>
> —Koko T., Seventh Grade

5. **Keep up on pedagogy.** Don't just keep current with how to communicate your content, but challenge yourself to look ahead at the ways people are presenting information. Remember when word clouds first came on the scene? Or infographics? What about screencasting? Be fearless in trying new ways to present your content and new ways students can present their learning. It's not that you can't use age-old and tried-and-true methods, but just keep in mind that other teachers are using them each year as well.

6. **Bring the students into the teaching.** Let's face it; you have 30–40 different brains in your classroom that might be looking at the material in a new way. Teach the students to be teachers. Jigsaw the concept you want to teach so that students are put in charge of communicating the concept themselves. Believe me, they will come at it in ways totally different than that which you would do. They'll help their peers understand a concept in a different voice and even bring in different resources to relate to the material. Have students bring in examples from the world outside of school that aligns with the concept you are trying to teach. Invite other brains to the table.

ENGAGING TEACHER SPOTLIGHT

Jennifer Trapp, EdD, is a current middle school teacher who specializes in project-based learning and cross-curricular unit development. In the following unit, she helps students understand and empathize with Holocaust survivors by moving beyond the textbook and introducing students to something new: the voices of the survivors themselves.

OVERVIEW

Middle and high school students will take a unique approach to learning about the Holocaust by centering their inquiry on survivor and eyewitness testimonies from the USC Shoah Foundation's Visual History Archive Online (https://sfi.usc.edu/). Following the

Group Investigation model of teaching, the learning path begins with the voices of the Holocaust and allows the testimonies to inspire student engagement in a collaborative inquiry process. Students strive to answer their research questions and corroborate testimonies by investigating additional primary and secondary sources. When presenting their findings, students honor the voices of Holocaust survivors and witnesses by incorporating them into their presentations. The lesson concludes with groups evaluating their learning process and determining which questions merit further investigation.

LESSON OBJECTIVE

- Students will conduct collaborative research to corroborate testimonies from survivors and witnesses of the Holocaust, and present their findings to their peers.

LESSON SEQUENCE

STEP 1: PRESENT THE PROBLEM

The teacher "presents the problem" by screening a video of a Holocaust survivor's testimony. The teacher refrains from introductory remarks and allows the testimony to spark students' interest and engagement. Students are allowed to draw or write as they watch the testimony to capture their reactions to the survivor and topic.

STEP 2: SOLICIT STUDENT QUESTIONS

After viewing the testimony, the teacher neutrally solicits student questions about what they watched and learned. These questions are recorded on the board for the entire class to see. Questions range from specifics about the survivor's testimony, to the Holocaust, and to WWII more broadly. The class groups the questions into categories.

STEP 3: RESEARCH

Students form research groups based on their interest in the question categories. Each research group is responsible for investigating and answering all the questions in one category.

The groups develop research plans to investigate their research questions and assign roles to group members. Throughout the research process, the teacher acts as advisor and consultant by answering student questions, helping them navigate the complexities of historical investigation, and curating a rich list of resources. Careful to guide students back to testimonies and other primary sources, the teacher challenges students to corroborate sources and construct an understanding of history from the voices and perspectives of those who experienced the Holocaust.

STEP 4: SHARE FINDINGS

After conducting extensive research, the groups then prepare a presentation of their findings. The presentations incorporate testimonies and other primary sources to answer research questions.

STEP 5: EVALUATE

Groups collaboratively determine how they will evaluate their work. Some groups create checklists documenting their efforts, some write narrative reflections, others create and complete rubrics.

STEP 6: RECYCLE

The final step is for the class to determine which questions from the first testimony merit further investigation and what additional questions emerged from the research process. Inevitably, students want to investigate other examples of genocide in history.

REFLECTION ON STUDENT ENGAGEMENT

The combination of focusing historical study on survivor testimony with the Group Investigation model of teaching leads to high levels of personal and collaborative engagement in the learning process. The students are moved by the powerful voices of the Holocaust survivors and are inspired to investigate the context and circumstances leading to the Holocaust. Since students are proposing the research questions and then selecting their groups, intrinsic motivation is increased as students become invested in the collaborative inquiry process.

DISCUSSION QUESTIONS

1. When was the last time you brought a new kind of artifact into the classroom that the students can produce? When was the last time you introduced students to a new method of communicating your content area?

2. How much time do you spend in your classroom on testing (federal, state, district, department, or classroom) and test prep? What percentage of your time is spent on testing and test prep?

3. Are there other voices you can bring into the classroom (or find within your classroom) that can help present material so that it comes with a fresh perspective?

4. Think of your favorite, albeit more traditionally crafted, lesson. How might you modify this beloved lesson to bring in a technique that is both new to you and new to the students?

Photo courtesy of Davis Lester

CHAPTER NINE

MIX THINGS UP

"It is so boring when we do the same thing over and over again."

OVERVIEW

This chapter covers one of the most frequently mentioned responses on the survey: mixing up the methods of teaching rather than merely focusing on one. Teaching should be like a braid, one that weaves together many strategies.

Sure, it's valuable to have different teachers become experts in one method or another; that creates a great

"I also feel engaged when a teacher does something different every couple times we do it. It is so boring when we do the same thing over and over again."

—Christy T.

diversity of implementation on a school site. But what students are requesting is that each teacher also embed a diversity of strategies in their classrooms as well, that they become adept in many different strategies of implementation so that day-to-day learning can become a melting pot of methods and outcomes.

"I enjoy it when there is variety in what we do, like a reading activity one day, and then an art thing the next day. Projects also are a great way to keep me engaged, I get to work with a group and show my understanding of the material in the best way that I can. When a lesson shows its importance in the real world around us, it really makes it seem like I should pay attention even more, to get the most out of it. Hands on things are truly the best for my attention, whether it's using technology or using motions to help us remember things. Choices can help students (like me) be more successful, because we know what we will do the best on."

—Margot D.

Not sure what strategy works best for your students? Try them all. Sample the snack bowls on the table, those full of engaging and rigorous strategies that bring your students' smiles and brains to the table. And when their smiles are at play, so are yours. After all, an offshoot of focusing on student engagement is that the teacher is also engaged. Sure the enjoyment of learning is trickle down, from teacher to student, but without a doubt, seeing your students engaged also rubs off on you.

"Not sure what strategy works best for your students? Try them all. Sample the snack bowls on the table."

LEARNING STYLES VERSUS MULTIPLE INTELLIGENCES

As educators, we talk about different learning styles. We talk about the ways in which all of our students learn and the way we best approach our work. I've known some teachers to assess their own students to "see" their learning styles as a means to help them somehow reach those kids. If anyone is to be assessed, however, I believe it should be the teachers themselves so that it might indicate to each individual teacher the strategies toward which we repeatedly gravitate. But I digress.

There are arguments for and against the existence of learning styles. Some believe that there really is no objective scientific research to back up the claim that we approach learning with different tendencies ("Learning Styles Challenged," 2009). Researcher Howard Gardner would push back that an "[a]bsence of evidence does not prove non-existence of a phenomenon; it signals to educational researchers: 'back to the drawing boards'" (Gardner, 2013). But for those who buy-in to the fact that people have ways in which they approach their goals differently, we are generally talking about a foundational three categories of styles. We ask ourselves and our students if they are any of the following:

> "I'm also more engaged when learning comes in many different forms (visuals, videos, etc.)."
>
> —Anthony V.

Visual—Do they respond better if they see it?

Auditory—Do they respond better if they hear it?

Kinesthetic—Do they respond better if they move while doing it?

Additionally, we talk about different modalities of learning as well, categories that represent different aptitudes. Modalities shift their focus from how we best tackle work to what we are inherently apt in. Edutopia writes,

> "I am engaged when my teachers show examples in multiple ways so that I can figure out which way makes the most sense."
>
> —Dylan G., Sixth Grade

The theory of *multiple intelligences* challenges the idea of a single IQ, where human beings have one central "computer" where intelligence is housed. Howard Gardner, the Harvard professor who originally proposed the theory, says that there are multiple types of human intelligence, each representing different ways of processing information. ("Multiple Intelligences," 2013)

We all have some aptitude in everything. For this reason, we often see the multiple intelligences represented as a pie chart with pieces labeled for each identified intelligence and each "slice" filled in at varying levels, as shown in Figure 9.1.

"Personally, I do like lecture classes, but they aren't the classes that get my attention. Classes that get my attention are classes that incorporate all different learning styles. Classes that have video and audio lessons as well as hands on lesson keep me engaged and an active part of the classroom. Having different types of assignments also keeps me engaged. Going for a group project to a whole class game to an individual work sheet back to a lecture and then another project is a cycle that helps me learn the material withou just taking copious amounts of notes."

—Lola B., Eleventh Grade

We have abilities that might be reflected in all eight categories, but we are more able in some than in others. We know how vital it is to include lessons implemented in different ways. It's about leaving drill-and-kill worksheets behind and utilizing all kinds of strategies. As the *Position Statement on Multimodal Literacies* by

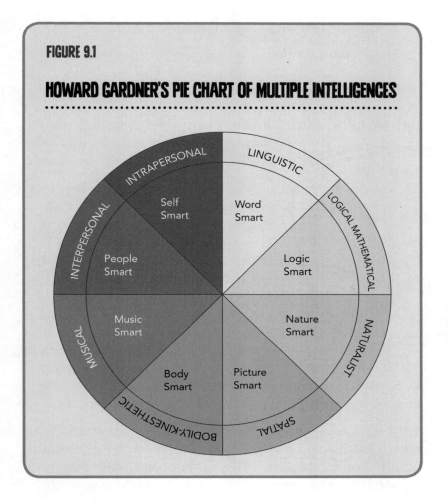

FIGURE 9.1

HOWARD GARDNER'S PIE CHART OF MULTIPLE INTELLIGENCES

NCTE (2005) states, "Multiple ways of knowing also include art, music, movement, and drama, which should not be considered curricular luxuries."

Despite the frequency of use in both of these theories, and despite their intentions to help guide teachers, they can also serve to freeze students in different labels. By assessing ourselves and our students, and learning their style or modality, the risk is that it may shove both us and them into that one category.

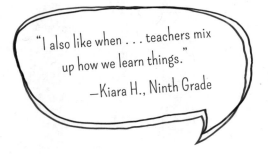

"I also like when . . . teachers mix up how we learn things."

—Kiara H., Ninth Grade

For that reason, Howard Gardner, the father of multiple intelligences theory, begged practitioners to focus on three points:

1. Individualize teaching—learn what you can about each student and teach in ways that encourage comfort.

2. Pluralize teaching—teach materials in a variety of ways.

3. Stop using the term *styles*. (Strauss, 2013)

And it seems the students agree. After all, many of the students who responded to the engagement survey pushed that despite what their tendencies and our tendencies may reveal, what they really want is access to many strategies, many ways of learning the content, and many ways of showing what they've learned.

> "I think that a classroom where the styles of teaching and how we learn the material changes constantly so that it keeps you engaged. Also if you don't like the one particular style of teaching it is fine because it will change soon."
>
> —Irwin F., Twelfth Grade

When teachers deliver material (or ask that students present their learning) in only one way, it can challenge a student's engagement. After all, according to Carol Ann Tomlinson in *How to Differentiate Instruction in Mixed-Ability Classrooms*, "Sometimes schools [feel like] a shoe shaped for somebody else's foot" (Tomlison, 2010, p. 10). Under the best of circumstances, there might be a student who relates to that one method of presentation or outcome, but even for that student, that one method can get boring.

What students are requesting taps into those theories but tackles them through a different lens. It's one thing to teach using visuals because there are visual learners in the classroom. It's one thing to use collaborative grouping because there are students who seek interpersonal experiences. But what we are talking about in this chapter is the need to mix up our delivery and utilize both of these strategies and more, because no matter how enthusiastic particular students may be with particular methods, any one of them, when not included in a deck of strategies, can get old quickly without variety. Tomlinson (2010) writes that there are "multiple avenues to learning," and these need to be blended in order to maintain engagement.

> "I always enjoy hands on learning. I like activities that are done in groups and require teamwork. I also like when teachers change their teaching styles. It gets very boring when you go into a class room and do the same thing everyday."
>
> —Melissa I., Eleventh Grade

Now, we all know that teaching using different styles and modalities can help a student feel comfortable with the process of learning, but learning isn't always about feeling comfortable. Deep learning should be about sweating, pushing, tearing mental muscles to rebuild tissue and think of things differently. Learning is about discomfort. According to Anthony G. Picciano's (n.d.) *Blending with Purpose: The Multimodal Model*, "A major benefit of multiple modalities is that they allow students to experience learning in ways in which they are most comfortable while also challenging them to experience and learn in other ways as well."

Want to really engage your students? Mix up your strategies, not only during a particular unit, but even during a particular lesson.

"There are many things that engage me as a student. I like learning things in many different ways. I think that learning topics and ideas in different ways helps to understand the subject better."

—Luz L., Tenth Grade

"No matter how enthusiastic particular students may be with particular methods, any one of them, when not included in a deck of strategies, can get old quickly without variety."

"What engages me during lessons are when the teacher does different types of activities. . . . I find that learning in the same way every lesson gets boring and I feel that I don't want to engage in the subject."

—Karen D., Eighth Grade

ENGAGE WITH THE CONTENT!

In this video, middle school math teacher, Susie Aames weaves multiple strategies into her lessons. The result is a super-engaging classroom that allows her to focus on the individual needs of her students. As you watch, notice the following:

- How does she leverage peer teaching to accomplish tasks?
- What are students doing as she gives 1:1 time with individual students?
- When are students working independently and collaboratively?

Video 9.1 Mix It Up

WHAT MIXING UP OUR IMPLEMENTATION LOOKS LIKE IN THE CLASSROOM

Throughout this book, we've covered different ways a teacher can engage his or her students. Just to review, we've looked at the following:

- Collaboration and community building
- Making lessons more visual and utilizing technology
- Building units that are more meaningful through project-based learning
- Designing more kinesthetic lessons
- Giving students choice
- Being more human with our students and sharing our own growth mindset
- Creating something with the content
- Opening up students' eyes to new concepts and topics

> "One thing that engages me as a student is when a teacher doesn't do the same thing over and over. I prefer it to be slightly different everyday."
>
> —Yarelly H., Middle Schooler

> "It is also nice when teachers change up how they teach instead of the same old 'take notes everyday' method."
>
> —Brian J., Twelfth Grade

The goal is to blend these, weaving them together so that more students are engaged more often. In some ways, you are capitalizing on what Dr. Judy Willis (n.d) calls, "syn-naps," the act of surprising the brain into awareness by jolting it awake, many times by transitioning to another modality.

There are so many combinations of strategies that a teacher can use in the classroom at any given time and for any given subject.

Try this. Check out the Student Engagement Playing Cards in Figures 9.2 and 9.3. With them, you can design lessons that use a combination of engagement strategies.

There are two sets:

Implementation—These are meant to inspire a variety of ways to help a student learn.

Outcome—These are meant to encourage a variety of ways in which a student might show their learning.

FIGURE 9.2

IMPLEMENTATION ENGAGEMENT CARDS

Warm-Up

Mini-Lesson

Student Work

Informal Assessment/Exit Card

Implementation **Collaboration: Small-group work** **(pairs).**	*Implementation* **Collaboration: Small-group work** **(3–5 students).**	*Implementation* **Use Visuals: Include a visual** **(video, image, etc.).**	*Implementation* **Use Technology: Include a sound bite** **(music, podcast, etc.).**
Implementation **PBL: Bring in an outside expert via Skype or face-to-face.**	*Implementation* **PBL: Have students role-play.**	*Implementation* **Kinesthetic: Time to move!** **Four-corner debate**	*Implementation* **Student Choice: Choose your topic.**
Implementation **Student Choice: Choose your resource.**	*Implementation* **Be Human: Share a story that relates to the topic.**	*Implementation* **Use Technology: Produce a screencast about your topic.**	*Implementation* **Something New: Find a clip from a TEDTalk or iTunes U.**

FIGURE 9.3

OUTCOME ENGAGEMENT CARDS

Outcome Collaboration: Gamify an informal assessment for group points using Kahoot.	*Outcome* Collaboration: Create a jigsaw essay or poster.	*Outcome* Visuals: Develop an infographic using Piktochart.	*Outcome* Use Technology: Develop a Google form to quiz their peers.
Outcome PBL: Develop a website to promote the topic.	*Outcome* PBL: Teach a lesson in the topic.	*Outcome* Student Choice: Let students pick how to show their learning.	*Outcome* Be Human: Reflect on what you don't understand and brainstorm next steps.
Outcome Create Something: Develop an invention that reflects the concept.	*Outcome* Something New: Bring in an article that mentions the concept.	*Outcome* Kinesthetic: Conduct a gallery walk through student artifacts.	*Outcome* Visual: Develop a storyboard sequencing how you learned the topic using the program Storyboard That!

They represent just a few methods you can use; but there are so many more that qualify under the student engagement criteria. Think about your content and shuffle the deck. Use the following lesson structure to insert any number of methods of delivery or outcomes into your lesson planning and design.

So by using the above lesson structure and a deck of Student Engagement cards, a particular class might look like the following:

MATH: CONCEPT—SUBTRACTING DECIMALS

Warm-Up: Use a visual—Show a BrainPop video on subtracting decimals.

Mini-Lesson: PBL—Have students role-play as a curator for an auction house and decide on prices for a list of items to be sold.

Student Work: Collaboration—Have students work in groups to run a mock-auction with one student as the auctioneer and the others "bidding." Give students fake bank accounts and have them add and subtract in a ledger as they bid on the items.

Informal Assessment/Exit Card: Something new—Each student brings in an ad that includes a decimal.

"It's important that student have time to study in many way. I think when teachers explain in many way is a good way to do. Because sometimes I don't understand at all."

—Mindy, Tenth Grade

"I am stronger in math thanks to my math teacher. Mr Tang teaches math lessons very well and lets us students understand it very quickly. When he teaches, he draws pictures, uses videos, and even uses a few "gaming" websites (of course educational related) and makes it better to comprehend. He also lets us do a lot of peer work which is really great because we can collaborate with other students and think of new ideas. In his class, we also do a few projects. Mr Tang doesn't assign projects for us to just do work. He always has a reason which is either to help us or to build our skill and knowledge."

—Wiltur C., Seventh Grade

LANGUAGE ARTS: CONCEPT—EMBEDDING EVIDENCE INTO A PERSUASIVE ESSAY

Warm-Up: Student choice—Students are given a choice of websites and articles to sift through looking for examples of ways evidence is embedded into the writing.

Mini-Lesson: PBL—Have the editor of a local college newspaper skype into the classroom to talk about what kinds of stories get approved for page 1.

Student Work: Collaboration—Have students create a Jigsaw Essay with each student developing a paragraph in the essay and each paragraph using embedded evidence within it.

Informal Assessment/Exit Card: Kinesthetic—Conduct a gallery walk through student artifacts.

ENGAGING TEACHER SPOTLIGHT

I thought I'd end this book with a surprise guest in our final Engaging Teacher Spotlight: You.

Check out this following activity to help you plan a lesson that reflects multiple engagement strategies. I've broken down the activity into three parts, much like the other teachers spotlighted in this book: Overview, Step-by-Step guide, and Reflection. Furthermore, I've broken down the step-by-step through the lesson into three simple parts, much like telling a story. After all, developing curriculum is a narrative in how students learn. The three parts are as follows:

- Introduction
- Body
- Conclusion

Look to this activity when you need a reminder that it's possible to braid methods of implementation, all in an attempt to lure students to learning.

YOUR MIX-IT-UP LESSON

Grade Level Taught: _____

Subject Area Focus: _____

Additional Skills Required: _____

Engagement Word Bank:

1. Collaboration   2. Community Building

                3. Making Lessons More Visual

                                    4. Utilizing Technology

        5. Role Play

                                        6. Real-World Application

                        7. Kinesthetic

8. Student Choice

                                        9. Modeling Growth Mindset

                        10. Creating With Content

                                            11. New Material

12. New Resource

                            13. New Tool

Now, you have a choice in how to develop your mixed-up lesson:

You can develop the lesson you have in your head and identify the strategies already being used. Then, look back at gaps that can be addressed to see if you can make it even more mixed up.

or

You can develop the lesson with the strategies in mind as you go. Strategize with the implementation and output in mind.

OVERVIEW

Write a short paragraph to put your lesson in context. How does it fit into the scheme of things in terms of both content knowledge and engagement?

_____

_____

_____

_____

_____

_____

STEP-BY-STEP GUIDE

Introduction: Describe in one to two sentences what you want students to learn and how you will present it. Will they be watching something? Reading something? Listening to something? Playing something? Will you use yourself and your life's story as an example of this content?

_____

_____

_____

_____

_____

_____

_____

Engagement Strategy(ies) Number Used (see box above): _____

_____

Body: Describe in one to two sentences what the students will be doing to practice this skill. Will they be working in groups? Will they talk to each other? Will they develop a collaborative slideshow or poster? Will students be able to choose their resources? Will students be using their bodies and movement to model the content?

_____

_____

_____

_____

_____

(Continued)

(Continued)

_____

_____

Engagement Strategy(ies) Number Used (see box above): _____

_____

Conclusion: Describe in one to two sentences how the students will show what they can do. Will they be producing an artifact? A recording? An infographic? A campaign? A page in a digital portfolio? What will they create with what they learned?

_____

_____

_____

_____

_____

Engagement Strategy(ies) Number Used (see box above): _____

_____

REFLECTION
· ·

Come back to this section once you have done your lesson. How did it go? What did you notice about your students' level of engagement? Did it help them achieve the goals of the lesson? Did they fall short in the quality of what they produced or exceed all expectations? How did their engagement engage you? In this space, you can share what worked and what didn't and how to make the implementation and execution better. What comes next?

_____

_____

_____

_____

_____

This Engaging Teacher Spotlight Lesson is available for you to download on the companion website at http://resources.corwin.com/justaskus.

Photo courtesy of Davis Lester

CONCLUSION

As we wrap up our tour of various engagement strategies, I want to reiterate some key points and leave you with a couple of new things to think about as well. For one, I hope that you've come away from this book ditching the myth that engaging also means you have to be on stage all day. I hope you've moved on from thinking that engagement must always mean that your lessons have to be fun.

Admittedly, however, when lessons are engaging, effort becomes enjoyable. It's a lot like playing a sport, coming off a field smiling and sweating and breathing hard. Brains can sweat too.

But I also hope that you've realized that this menu of strategies doesn't mean you have to order them all to have a full meal of engagement. Look over your current lessons. Pick and choose what strategies of engagement might be best to add as a layer in order to address your standards, support your students, and work within your school's constraints. Some strategies might feel like a stretch for one lesson but totally organic for another. If you commit to just dipping your toe into a couple of them, you will be further along on your own journey to be an engaging teacher.

Now, I understand that it might seem that even adopting a couple of strategies can be hard. In fact, I totally agree that pushing yourself out of your own wheelhouse or targeting these strategies more frequently can be challenging. But it's worth it.

IT'S HARD TO BE ENGAGING

Look, I'll be frank: It's a lot easier to be a teacher who doesn't focus on engagement. And teaching is a difficult job as it is. Even if your idea of implementation is more whole class than small group; even if your classroom is driven more by worksheet than workshops; even if you are far more comfortable lecturing than letting them move around, it's a challenging job.

But using engagement strategies to lure kids into learning, while it seems draining, is an investment in your own energy as an educator. Being engaging as a teacher—thinking about engagement and challenging yourself to teach the students in different ways—is not just an investment in students; it's also an investment in you and your quality of life.

So now I'll let you in on a little secret: I neglected to mention something vital about student engagement earlier in this book. Remember when I told you that engagement trickles down? That if you are engaged, then your students will be too?

Well, that wasn't a lie, but I did leave something out of that statement. The fact is that engagement is cyclical. If your students are engaged, you will be too. See, student engagement acts like a teacher's batteries. The students' eureka moments, their excitement, their discoveries and efforts, recharge you. And much like your phone gets a new boost of energy after you slap on a spare charger, so do you get a new surge of engagement for each day the students are engaged.

> "And much like your phone gets a new boost of energy after you slap on a spare charger, so do you get a new surge of engagement for each day the students are engaged."

In other words, students and teachers are interdependent. We are the water buffalo to their egrets. We are binary stars that orbit each other.

And just as the needs of our clients have evolved, so must we.

It's as much about what is right to do as it is about doing our job right. We can't help our students without using engagement strategies. We as a profession are competing for these kids' attention with so many other outside elements. We are competing against social media and Netflix. We are competing against having crushes and getting dumped. We are competing against hunger and homelessness, bullying, and abuse. We are competing against the changes happening and the fears of those ahead. We compete against elements in our students' lives that range from traumatic to simply more interesting, and those elements will win out—unless we prove to be more engaging.

It's become a part of our job to not only teach the content, but to teach it in a way that stands a chance against the competition.

ENGAGE WITH THE CONTENT!

The video footage to the right expands more on being an engaged teacher. Think about those times when student engagement also helped motivate you. Think about what triggered those moments and how the cycle of engagement continues.

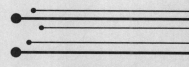

Video 10.1 Engage With Your Learners

And the only way to do it is to tackle our students' levels of engagement.

WHAT TO EXPECT WHEN YOU ADOPT THESE STRATEGIES

So what might you see once you embrace these student engagement strategies? In terms of learning outcomes, I've peppered some of that research throughout the book. Arguably as important, however, is what you can expect from the culture of your classroom quality and, as a result, what you can expect from your day-to-day existence as a teacher. So to answer this question, let's think about this concretely.

WHAT DOES ENGAGEMENT LOOK LIKE?

I would expect more eureka moments. Now, we're not just talking about the occasional light bulb; we're talking about strobe lights. I would expect more smiles. I would also expect deeper lines of concentration, for students who are engaged persist. Students who are engaged plow through greater challenges than those who are not.

I would also take a look at yourself in this scenario. My guess is that you are working more 1:1 with students or with small groups because other groups are more on-task due to engagement. My guess is that you are being drawn into more conversations and your own smile is a fixture in the room as well.

WHAT DOES ENGAGEMENT SOUND LIKE?

I would expect more sound, more talking, more sharing, a greater buzz. I would also expect more silence, more depth of processing. Metacognition, after all, is both loud at times and quiet in others.

In terms of yourself, you might be talking more with students, but their engagement might also be a cue for your own silence. You will be abdicating some of the authority to them, after all, and allowing them to choose, and to communicate, and to learn through doing. This means more guidance from you to help them seek answers, but less strenuous attempts to force the learning onto them.

WHAT DOES ENGAGEMENT FEEL LIKE?

I would expect that students are both excited and frustrated. They are excited because they are going down the rabbit hole of inquiry and student-centered approaches. They might be frustrated because engagement lures them into more rigorous learning, and they want to accomplish it more. With rigor comes brain sweat; and that's OK.

And you will feel more pride in them as you see your students grab the ring themselves. Through collaboration, movement, choice, and your own modeling, your students will step up and show you what they can do. Mix up your implementation, use visuals, guide them to create something from what they learn, and ensure they are indeed learning something new. In so doing, you will also feel excitement by seeing your classroom through their lens.

Without engagement, your students cannot absorb your content. Without engagement, your students will not be willing to go through the steps of the learning process. Without engagement, your students will not be on your side, and you are a vital ally in their development.

Adopt these strategies and you will have adopted a mindset that shows students you care about their future and about their own day-to-day existence as learners. You are in this together, and may it be a journey that is engaging to all.

REFERENCES

INTRODUCTION

Kashdan, T. (2010, April 13). Science shows you can die of boredom, literally. *The Huffington Post*. Retrieved March 21, 2017, from http://www.huffingtonpost.com/todd-kashdan/science-shows-you -can-die_b_457199.html

Kids speak out on student engagement. (2012, April 26). *Edutopia*. Retrieved February 10, 2017. https://www.edutopia.org/blog/ student-engagement-stories-heather-wolpert-gawron

Philip, R. T., 2006. *Engaging 'tweens and teens: A brain-compatible approach to reaching middle and high school students*. Thousand Oaks, CA: Corwin.

Willis, J. (n.d.). The neuroscience of joyful education. *Psychology Today*. Retrieved March 21, 2017, from https://www.psychologytoday .com/files/attachments/4141/the-neuroscience-joyful-education -judy-willis-md.pdf

CHAPTER 1

Center for Teaching Excellence (CTE). (n.d.). Collaborative learning. Cornell Center for Teaching Excellence. Retrieved January 30, 2017, from https://www.cte.cornell.edu/teaching-ideas/engaging -students/collaborative-learning.html

Darling-Hammond, L., & Barron, B. (2012, December 5). Research supports collaborative learning. *Edutopia*. Retrieved January 30, 2017, from https://www.edutopia.org/stw-collaborative-learning-research

Dotson, J. M. (2001, Winter). Cooperative learning structures can increase student achievement. *Kagan Online Magazine*. Retrieved March 23, 2017, from https://www.kaganonline.com/free_articles/research_and_rationale/increase_achievement.php

Emanuel, G. (2016, May 28). How to fix a graduation rate of 1 in 10? Ask the dropouts. *nprEd*. Retrieved January 30, 2017, from http://www.npr.org/sections/ed/2016/05/28/479208574/how-to-fix-a-graduation-rate-of-1-in-10-ask-the-dropouts

Johnson, D., & Johnson, R. (2004, March 24). Cooperative learning methods: A meta-analysis—ResearchGate. Retrieved March 23, 2017, from https://www.researchgate.net/profile/David_Johnson50/publication/220040324_Cooperative_learning_methods_A_meta-analysis/links/00b4952b39d258145c000000.pdf

Johnson, D. W., Johnson, R. T., & Johnson Holubec, E. (n.d.). The new circles of learning: Cooperation in the classroom. ASCD. Retrieved March 23, 2017, from http://www.ascd.org/publications/books/194034.aspx

National Education Association (NEA). (n.d.). Research spotlight on cooperative learning. Retrieved March 21, 2017, from http://www.nea.org/tools/16870.htm

Priebatsch, S. (2010). The game layer on top of the world. *TEDTalk*. Retrieved January 31, 2017, from https://www.ted.com/talks/seth_priebatsch_the_game_layer_on_top_of_the_world/transcript

Shaw, A. (2013, August 13). Back to school: A surefire strategy for building classroom community. Retrieved January 30, 2017, from https://www.edutopia.org/blog/back-to-school-strategy-building-community-anne-shaw

Slavin, R. E. (1996). Research on cooperative learning and achievement: What we know, what we need to know. *Contemporary Educational Psychology, 21,* 43–69. Retrieved from http://s3.amazonaws.com/academia.edu.documents/32134643/Cooperative_Learning_-_SLAVIN__Robert.pdf?AWSAccessKeyId=AKIAIWOWYYGZ2Y53UL3A&Expires=1490154117&Signature=B5o8Z2MbBUtYfh%2BfcHW9LCm9dEg%3D&response-content-disposition=inline%3B%20filename%3DRESEARCH_FOR_THE_FUTURE_Research_on_Coop.pdf

Wessing, S. B. (2012, September 10). 14 ways to cultivate classroom chemistry. Teaching Channel. Retrieved May 18, 2017, from https://www.teachingchannel.org/blog/2012/09/10/14-ways-to-cultivate-classroom-chemistry/

CHAPTER 2

Dale, E. (1969). Cone of experience. In R. V. Wiman, ed., *Educational media: Theory into practice*. Charles Merrill: Columbus, Ohio

Horn, R. E. (n.d.). Visual language and converging technologies in the next 10–15 years (and beyond). Retrieved February 10, 2017, from https://web.stanford.edu/~rhorn/a/recent/artclNSFVisualLangv.pdf

Kouyoumdjian, H. (2012, July 20). Learning through visuals. *Psychology Today*. Retrieved February 10, 2017, from https://www.psychologytoday.com/blog/get-psyched/201207/learning-through-visuals

McDaniel, M. A. (2015, June 17). Study: Students learn better when lectures come with visual aids. Blogs. Retrieved February 10, 2017, from http://blogs.edweek.org/teachers/teaching_now/2015/06/visual-diagrams-help-students-take-notes.html

Nussbaum-Beach, S. (2016, September 1). Best classroom uses of technology. Retrieved February 10, 2017, from http://plpnetwork.com/2016/09/01/best-classroom-uses-of-technology/

Schrotenboer, K. (2014, June 3). Visual technology fosters increased comprehension and retention for newly-empowered students. Retrieved February 10, 2017, from http://www.emergingedtech.com/2014/06/visual-technology-increases-comprehension-retention/

Using technology to create a visual learning environment. (n.d.). *Colorín*. Retrieved February 10, 2017, from http://www.colorincolorado.org/article/using-technology-create-visual-learning-environment

Visual Teaching Alliance. (n.d.). Retrieved February 10, 2017, from http://visualteachingalliance.com/

CHAPTER 3

Bentley, J. (2016, December 18). Personal communication.

Boaler, J. (2002, July). Exploring the relationship between reform curriculum and equity. *Journal for Research in Mathematics Education, 33*(4), 239–258. Retrieved March 31, 2017, from https://www.jstor.org/stable/749740

The difference between projects and project-based learning. (2012, December 3). Retrieved April 4, 2017, from http://www.teachthought.com/learning/project-based-learning/difference-between-projects-and-project-based-learning/

Fruchter, R. (n.d.). Speaking of teaching. Stanford University. Retrieved February 10, 2017, from http://web.stanford.edu/dept/CTL/cgi-bin/docs/newsletter/motivation_to_learn.pdf

Holt. T. (2013, January 10). Why problem based learning is better—Powerful learning practice. Retrieved February 10, 2017, from http://plpnetwork.com/2013/01/10/problem-vs-project-based-learning/

Miller, A. (2012, May 3). Six affirmations for PBL teachers. *Edutopia*. Retrieved February 10, 2017, from https://www.edutopia.org/blog/affirmations-for-pbl-teachers-andrew-miller

National Education Association. (n.d.). Research spotlight on project-based learning. Retrieved February 10, 2017, from http://www.nea.org/tools/16963.htm

Strobel, J., & van Barneveld, A. (2009). When is PBL more effective? A meta-synthesis of meta-analyses comparing PBL to conventional classrooms. Retrieved March 31, 2017, from http://docs.lib.purdue.edu/ijpbl/vol3/iss1/4/

U.S. Department of Education. (2011). Effects of problem based economics on high school economics. Retrieved March 31, 2017, from https://ies.ed.gov/ncee/edlabs/projects/project.asp?ProjectID=89

Vega, V. (2012, December 3). Project-based learning research review. *Edutopia*. Retrieved February 10, 2017, from https://www.edutopia.org/pbl-research-learning-outcomes

White, H. (n.d.). Speaking of teaching. Stanford University. Retrieved February 10, 2017, from http://web.stanford.edu/dept/CTL/cgi-bin/docs/newsletter/motivation_to_learn.pdf

Wilhelm, J., Dr. (2016, December 13). Teaching literacy for love and wisdom to help students meet and exceed the common core standards: From being the book to being the change. Speech presented at UCI Writing Project Conference in UCI Student Union, Irvine

Wolpert-Gawron, H. (2016, August 11). What the heck is inquiry-based learning? *Edutopia*. Retrieved February 10, 2017, from https://www.edutopia.org/blog/what-heck-inquiry-based-learning-heather-wolpert-gawron

CHAPTER 4

Beers, G. K., & Probst, R. E. (2016). *Reading nonfiction: Notice and note stances, signposts, and strategies*. Portsmouth, NH: Heinemann.

CDC. (2010). The association between school-based physical activity, including physical education, and academic performance. Retrieved March 17, 2017, from https://www.cdc.gov/healthyyouth/health_and_academics/pdf/pa-pe_paper.pdf

Green Gilbert, A. (1997). Movement is the key to learning. Retrieved March 17, 2017, from http://education.jhu.edu/PD/newhorizons/strategies/topics/Arts%20in%20Education/gilbert.htm

Jensen, E. (2005). Chapter 4. Movement and learning. ASCD. Retrieved January 28, 2017, from http://www.ascd.org/publications/books/104013/chapters/Movement-and-Learning.aspx

Levine, J. (2015). Sitting risks: How harmful is too much sitting? Mayo Clinic. Retrieved January 28, 2017, from http://www.mayoclinic.org/healthy-lifestyle/adult-health/expert-answers/sitting/faq-20058005

Rhodes, J. (2017). Why do I think better after I exercise? *Scientific American*. Retrieved January 28, 2017, from https://www.scientificamerican.com/article/why-do-you-think-better-after-walk-exercise/

Sims, R. R., & Sims, S. J. (1995). *The importance of learning styles: Understanding the implications for learning, course design, and education*. Westport, CT: Greenwood Press.

CHAPTER 5

Bentley, J. (2016, December 18). Personal communication.

Davis, S. L. (2016, September 13). The conundrum of student choice in project based learning. Retrieved February 10, 2017, from https://www.bie.org/blog/the_conundrum_of_student_choice_in_project_based_learning

Goodwin, B. (2010). Research says... /Choice is a matter of degree. ASCD. Retrieved February 10, 2017, from http://www.ascd.org/publications/educational-leadership/sept10/vol68/num01/Choice-Is-a-Matter-of-Degree.aspx

Khon, A. (2010, December 22). Why and how to let students decide. The IDEA Library. Retrieved February 10, 2017, from http://democraticeducation.org/index.php/library/resource/why_and_how_to_let_students_decide1/

Marzano Research. (n.d.). The highly engaged classroom, tips. Retrieved February 10, 2017, from https://www.marzanoresearch.com/resources/tips/hec_tips_archive

Patall, E. A., Cooper, H., Robinson, J. C. (n.d.). The effects of choice on intrinsic motivation and related outcomes. NCBI. Retrieved March 23, 2017, from https://www.ncbi.nlm.nih.gov/pubmed/18298272

Patall, E. A., Cooper, H., & Wynn, S. R. (2010). The effectiveness and relative importance of choice in the classroom. *Journal of Educational Psychology, 102*(4), 896–915. Retrieved from http://psycnet.apa.org/psycarticles/2010-19093-001

Starbucks stays mum on drink math—The numbers. (2008, April 2). *WSJ*. Retrieved February 10, 2017, from http://blogs.wsj.com/numbers/starbucks-stays-mum-on-drink-math-309/

CHAPTER 6

Australian Council for Educational Research. (2015, March 2). The teacher workforce in Australia: Supply, demand and data issues. Retrieved February 10, 2017, from http://research.acer.edu.au/cgi/viewcontent.cgi?article=1001&context=policyinsights

Dweck, C. (2014). The power of believing that you can improve [Transcript]. Retrieved February 10, 2017, from http://www.ted.com/talks/carol_dweck_the_power_of_believing_that_you_can_improve/transcript

Dweck, C. S., & Sorich Blackwell, L. (n.d.). Retrieved March 30, 2017, from https://www.mindsetworks.com/page/increase-students-motivation-grades-and-achievement-test-scores

Garner, R. (2016, February 29). Most secondary schools 'use teachers not trained in their subject.' *The Independent*. Retrieved February 10, 2017, from http://www.independent.co.uk/news/education/education-news/secondary-school-pupils-taught-by-staff-not-trained-in-their-subject-a6903996.html

Gehlbach, H., Brinkworth, M. E., King, A. M., Hsu, L. M. McIntyre, J., & Rogers, T. (In press). *Creating birds of similar feathers*. Amazon Web Services. Retrieved February 10, 2017, from https://panorama-www.s3.amazonaws.com/research/similarity.pdf

Marci, C. (2010, June 28). Humor, laughter, and those aha moments. Retrieved February 10, 2017, from https://hms.harvard.edu/news/humor-laughter-and-those-aha-moments-6-28-10

Morrison, M. K. (2008). *Using humor to maximize learning: The links between positive emotions and education*. Rowman & Littlefield: Lanham, MD.

Muller, R. M. (2008). The influence of teachers' caring behavior on high school students' behavior and grades. Retrieved February 10, 2017, from http://scholarship.shu.edu/cgi/viewcontent.cgi?article=2636&context=dissertations

National Center for Education Statistics. (n.d.). Schools and staffing survey. Retrieved February 10, 2017, from https://nces.ed.gov/surveys/sass/tables/sass1112_2016003_t1s.asp

National Educational Association (NEA). (n.d.). A quality teacher is a caring teacher. Retrieved February 10, 2017, from http://www.nea.org/tools/15751.htm

Pegg, S. (n.d.). Retrieved February 10, 2017, from http://www.goodreads.com/quotes/556142-being-a-geek-is-all-about-being-honest-about-what

Rogers, T. (2017). Abstract. HKS Research Administration Office—Harvard University. Retrieved February 10, 2017, from https://research.hks.harvard.edu/publications/workingpapers/citation.aspx?PubId=9721&type=WPN

Stambor, Z. (2006, June). How laughing leads to learning. *Monitor Staff,* *37*(6), 62. Retrieved February 10, 2017, from http://www.apa.org/ monitor/jun06/learning.aspx

Wolpert-Gawron, H. (2014, September 26). The power of "I don't know." Retrieved February 10, 2017, from https://www.edutopia .org/blog/power-i-dont-know-heather-wolpert-gawron

CHAPTER 7

36 mind blowing YouTube facts, figures and statistics—2017. (2017). Retrieved April 3, 2017, from https://fortunelords.com/ youtube-statistics/

Camera, L. (2015, November 19). More schools have access to high-speed broadband than ever. Retrieved April 3, 2017, from https:// www.usnews.com/news/articles/2015/11/19/more-schools-have -access-to-high-speed-broadband-than-ever?offset=20

Center for Accelerated Learning. (n.d.). Retrieved April 3, 2017, from http://www.alcenter.com/what_is.php

Dark, M. (2009, January 28). Study: Hands-on projects may be best way to teach engineering and technology concepts. Retrieved April 3, 2017, from https://news.uns.purdue.edu/ x/2009a/090128DarkStudy.html

Ingmire, J. (2015, April 29). Learning by doing helps students perform better in science. Retrieved April 3, 2017, from https://news .uchicago.edu/article/2015/04/29/learning-doing-helps-students -perform-better-science

Shirkey, C. (2010, June). How cognitive surplus will change the world. *TEDTalk.* Retrieved April 3, 2017, from https://www.ted.com/ talks/clay_shirky_how_cognitive_surplus_will_change_the_world/ transcript

Somerville, M., & Goldberg, D. (2012, November 19). From consumption to creation: A new way to think about ownership in engineering education. *The Huffington Post.* Retrieved April 3, 2017, from http://www.huffingtonpost.com/mark-somerville/ engineering-education_b_2100577.html

CHAPTER 8

Center for American Progress. (n.d.). Council of the Great City Schools. Retrieved April 3, 2017, from http://www.cgcs.org/

Chamorro-Premuzic, T. (2014, August 27). Curiosity is as important as intelligence. *Harvard Business Review.* Retrieved April 3, 2017, from https://hbr.org/2014/08/curiosity-is-as-important -as-intelligence

Johnston, H. (2012, March). The spiral curriculum—ERIC. Retrieved April 3, 2017, from http://files.eric.ed.gov/fulltext/ED538282.pdf

Long, C. (2013, October 7). 'Drill and kill' testing scrutinized at 2013 Education Nation Summit. Retrieved April 3, 2017, from http://neatoday.org/2013/10/07/drill-and-kill-testing-scrutinized-at-2013-education-nation-summit-2/

Rowe, C. (2014, July 1). Is test-prep teaching? It takes up 18 percent of school time. *The Seattle Times.* Retrieved April 3, 2017, from http://blogs.seattletimes.com/educationlab/2014/07/01/teacher-study-legislature-mccoy/

Strauss, V. (n.d.). Council of the Great City Schools. Retrieved April 3, 2017, from http://www.cgcs.org/

Strauss, V. (2015, November 19). Report: Time spent on standardized testing in schools is underestimated. Retrieved April 3, 2017, from https://www.washingtonpost.com/news/answer-sheet/wp/2015/11/19/report-time-spent-on-standardized-testing-in-schools-is-underestimated/

Wolpert-Gawron, H. (2016, February 11). What the heck is all the whoop-dee-do with 3D printing? Edutopia. Retrieved April 3, 2017, from https://www.edutopia.org/blog/what-heck-all-whoop-dee-do-3d-printing-heather-wolpert-gawron

CHAPTER 9

Gardner, H. (2013, October 16). "Multiple intelligences" are not "learning styles." Retrieved January 31, 2017, from https://www.washingtonpost.com/news/answer-sheet/wp/2013/10/16/howard-gardner-multiple-intelligences-are-not-learning-styles/

Learning styles challenged. (2009, December 16). Association for Psychological Science. Retrieved January 31, 2017, from http://www.psychologicalscience.org/media/releases/2009/learningstylespspi.cfm

Multiple intelligences: What does the research say? (2013, March 8). Retrieved January 31, 2017, from https://www.edutopia.org/multiple-intelligences-research

NCTE position statement. (2005, November). Retrieved January 31, 2017, from http://www.ncte.org/positions/statements/multimodalliteracies

Picciano, A. G. (n.d.). Blending with purpose: The multimodal model. Retrieved January 31, 2017, from http://www.york.cuny.edu/academics/academic-affairs/assets/Blended%20Learning.pdf

Strauss, V. (2013, October 16). Howard Gardner: "Multiple intelligences" are not "learning styles." Retrieved January 31, 2017, from https://www.washingtonpost.com/news/answer-sheet/wp/2013/10/16/howard-gardner-multiple-intelligences-are-not-learning-styles/

Tomlinson, C. A. (2001). How to differentiate instruction in mixed-ability classrooms (2nd ed.). Alexandria, VA: ASCD. Retrieved January 31, 2017, from http://www.ascd.org/Publications/Books/Overview/How-to-Differentiate-Instruction-in-Mixed-Ability-Classrooms-2nd-Edition.aspx

Willis, J. (n.d.). Retrieved January 31, 2017, from http://www.radteach.com/

INDEX

A SAGE Publishing Company

CORWIN HAS ONE MISSION: to enhance education through intentional professional learning.

We build long-term relationships with our authors, educators, clients, and associations who partner with us to develop and continuously improve the best evidence-based practices that establish and support lifelong learning.

The Association for Middle Level Education is dedicated to improving the educational experiences of all students ages 10 to 15 by providing vision, knowledge, and resources to educators and leaders.